1-

CROCK·POT

·THE ORIGINAL SLOW COOKER·

COMFORT FOODS

pil

Publications International, Ltd.

TABLE OF CONTENTS

CLASSIC BEEF
AND NOODLES
PAGE 124

PASTA FAGIOLI SOUP
PAGE 10

SLOW COOKING 101

SIZES OF CROCK-POT®
SLOW COOKERS

Smaller **CROCK-POT®** slow cookers—such as 1- to 3½-quart models—are the perfect size for cooking for singles, a couple, or empty nesters (and also for serving dips).

While medium-size **CROCK-POT®** slow cookers (those holding somewhere between 3 quarts and 5 quarts) will easily cook enough food at one time to feed a small family. They are also convenient for holiday side dishes or appetizers.

Large **CROCK-POT®** slow cookers are great for large family dinners, holiday entertaining, and potluck suppers. A 6- to 7-quart model is ideal if you like to make meals in advance. Or, have dinner tonight and store leftovers for later.

TYPES OF CROCK-POT®
SLOW COOKERS

Current **CROCK-POT®** slow cookers come equipped with many different features and benefits, from auto cook programs to oven-safe stoneware to timed programming. Please visit **WWW.CROCK-POT.COM** to find the

CROCK-POT® slow cooker that best suits your needs.

How you plan to use a **CROCK-POT®** slow cooker may affect the model you choose to purchase. For everyday cooking, choose a size large enough to serve your family. If you plan to use the **CROCK-POT®** slow cooker primarily for entertaining, choose one of the larger sizes. Basic **CROCK-POT®** slow cookers can hold as little as 16 ounces or as much as 7 quarts. The smallest sizes are great for keeping dips warm on a buffet, while the larger sizes can more readily fit large quantities of food and larger roasts.

COOKING, STIRRING, AND FOOD SAFETY

CROCK-POT® slow cookers are safe to leave unattended. The outer heating base may get hot as it cooks, but it should not pose a fire hazard. The heating element in the heating base functions at a low wattage and is safe for your countertops.

Your **CROCK-POT®** slow cooker should be filled about one-half to three-fourths full for most recipes unless otherwise instructed. Lean meats such as chicken or pork tenderloin will cook faster than meats with more connective tissue and fat such as beef chuck or pork shoulder. Bone-in meats will take longer than boneless cuts. Typical **CROCK-POT®** slow cooker dishes take approximately 7 to 8 hours to reach the simmer point on LOW and about 3 to 4 hours on HIGH. Once the vegetables and meat start to simmer and braise, their flavors will fully blend and meat will become fall-off-the-bone tender.

According to the U.S. Department of Agriculture, all bacteria are killed at a temperature of 165°F. It's important to follow the recommended cooking times and not to open the lid often, especially early in the cooking process when heat is building up inside the unit. If you need to open the lid to check on your food or are adding additional ingredients, remember to allow additional cooking time if necessary to ensure food is cooked through and tender.

Large **CROCK-POT®** slow cookers, the 6- to 7-quart sizes, may benefit from a quick stir halfway through cook time to help distribute heat and promote even cooking. It's usually unnecessary to stir at all, as even ½ cup liquid will help to distribute heat and the stoneware is the perfect medium for holding food at an even temperature throughout the cooking process.

OVEN-SAFE STONEWARE

All **CROCK-POT®** slow cooker removable stoneware inserts may (without their lids) be used safely in ovens at up to 400°F. In addition, all **CROCK-POT®** slow cookers are microwavable without their lids. If you own another slow cooker brand, please refer to your owner's manual for specific stoneware cooking medium tolerances.

FROZEN FOOD

Frozen food can be successfully cooked in a **CROCK-POT®** slow cooker. However, it will require longer cooking time than the same recipe made with fresh food. Using an instant-read thermometer is recommended to ensure meat is fully cooked.

PASTA AND RICE

If you are converting a recipe for your **CROCK-POT**® slow cooker that calls for uncooked pasta, first cook the pasta on the stovetop just until slightly tender. Then add the pasta to the **CROCK-POT**® slow cooker. If you are converting a recipe for the **CROCK-POT**® slow cooker that calls for cooked rice, stir in raw rice with the other recipe ingredients plus ¼ cup extra liquid per ¼ cup of raw rice.

BEANS

Beans must be softened completely before combining with sugar and/or acidic foods in the **CROCK-POT**® slow cooker. Sugar and acid have a hardening effect on beans and will prevent softening. Fully cooked canned beans may be used as a substitute for dried beans.

VEGETABLES

Root vegetables often cook more slowly than meat. Cut vegetables accordingly to cook at the same rate as meat—large or small or lean versus marbled—and place near the sides or bottom of the stoneware to facilitate cooking.

HERBS

Fresh herbs add flavor and color when added at the end of the cooking cycle; if added at the beginning, many fresh herbs' flavor will dissipate over long cook times. Ground and/or dried herbs and spices work well in slow cooking and may be added at the beginning of cook time. For dishes with shorter cook times, hearty fresh herbs such as rosemary and thyme hold up well. The flavor power of all herbs and spices can vary greatly depending on their particular strength and shelf life. Use chili powders and garlic powder sparingly, as these can sometimes intensify over the long cook times. Always taste the finished dish and correct seasonings including salt and pepper.

LIQUIDS

It's not necessary to use more than ½ to 1 cup liquid in most instances since juices in meats and vegetables are retained more in slow cooking than in conventional cooking. Excess liquid can be cooked down and concentrated after slow cooking on the stovetop or by removing meat and vegetables from the stoneware, stirring in one of the following thickeners and setting the **CROCK-POT**® slow cooker to HIGH. Cover; cook on HIGH for approximately 15 minutes or until juices are thickened.

FLOUR: All-purpose flour is often used to thicken soups or stews. Stir water into the flour in a small bowl until smooth. With the **CROCK-POT**® slow cooker on HIGH, whisk flour mixture into the liquid in the **CROCK-POT**® slow cooker. Cover; cook on HIGH 15 minutes or until the mixture is thickened.

CORNSTARCH: Cornstarch gives sauces a clear, shiny appearance; it's used most often for sweet dessert sauces and stir-fry sauces. Stir water into the cornstarch in a small bowl until the cornstarch is dissolved. Quickly stir this mixture into the liquid in the **CROCK-POT**® slow cooker; the sauce will thicken as soon as the liquid simmers. Cornstarch breaks down with too much heat, so never add it at the beginning of the slow cooking process and turn off the heat as soon as the sauce thickens.

TAPIOCA: Tapioca is a starchy substance extracted from the root of the cassava plant. Its greatest advantage is that it withstands long cooking, making it an ideal choice for slow cooking. Add tapioca at the beginning of cooking and you'll get a clear, thickened sauce in the finished dish. Dishes using tapioca as a thickener are best cooked on the LOW setting; it may become stringy when boiled for a long time.

MILK

Milk, cream, and sour cream break down during extended cooking. When possible, add them during the last 15 to 30 minutes of slow cooking, until just heated through. Condensed soups may be substituted for milk and may cook for extended times.

FISH

Fish is delicate and should be stirred into the **CROCK-POT**® slow cooker gently during the last 15 to 30 minutes of cooking. Cover; cook just until cooked through and serve immediately.

BAKED GOODS

If you wish to prepare bread, cakes, or pudding cakes in a **CROCK-POT**® slow cooker, you may want to purchase a covered, vented metal cake pan accessory for your **CROCK-POT**® slow cooker. You can also use any straight-sided soufflé dish or deep cake pan that will fit into the stoneware of your unit. Baked goods can be prepared directly in the stoneware; however, they can be a little difficult to remove from the insert, so follow the recipe directions carefully.

MEATBALLS AND
SPAGHETTI SAUCE
PAGE 118

SOUPS, STEWS, AND CHILIES

WHITE CHICKEN CHILI

8 ounces dried navy
   beans, rinsed and
   sorted

1 tablespoon vegetable oil

2 pounds boneless,
   skinless chicken
   breasts (about 4)

2 onions, chopped

1 tablespoon minced
   garlic

2 teaspoons ground cumin

2 teaspoons salt

1 teaspoon dried oregano

¼ teaspoon black pepper

¼ teaspoon ground red
   pepper (optional)

4 cups chicken broth

1 can (4 ounces) fire-
   roasted diced mild
   green chiles, rinsed
   and drained

¼ cup chopped fresh
   cilantro

1 Place beans on bottom of **CROCK-POT**® slow cooker. Heat oil in large skillet over medium-high heat. Add chicken; cook 8 minutes or until browned on all sides. Remove to **CROCK-POT**® slow cooker.

2 Heat same skillet over medium heat. Add onions; cook 6 minutes or until softened and lightly browned. Add garlic, cumin, salt, oregano, black pepper and ground red pepper, if desired; cook and stir 1 minute. Add broth and chiles; bring to a simmer, stirring to scrape up any browned bits from bottom of skillet. Remove onion mixture to **CROCK-POT**® slow cooker.

3 Cover; cook on LOW 5 hours. Remove chicken to large cutting board; shred with two forks. Return chicken to **CROCK-POT**® slow cooker. Stir in cilantro.

MAKES 6 TO 8 SERVINGS

2 cans (about 14 ounces *each*) beef or vegetable broth

1 can (about 15 ounces) Great Northern beans, rinsed and drained

1 can (about 14 ounces) diced tomatoes

2 zucchini, quartered lengthwise and sliced

1 tablespoon olive oil

1½ teaspoons minced garlic

½ teaspoon dried basil

½ teaspoon dried oregano

½ cup uncooked ditalini, tubetti or small shell pasta

½ cup garlic-seasoned croutons

½ cup grated Asiago or Romano cheese

3 tablespoons chopped fresh basil or Italian parsley (optional)

1 Combine broth, beans, tomatoes, zucchini, oil, garlic, dried basil and oregano in **CROCK-POT**® slow cooker; stir to blend. Cover; cook on LOW 3 to 4 hours.

2 Stir in pasta. Cover; cook on LOW 1 hour or until pasta is tender. Serve soup with croutons and cheese. Garnish with fresh basil.

MAKES 5 TO 6 SERVINGS

TIP: Only small pasta varieties should be used in this recipe. The low heat of a **CROCK-POT**® slow cooker will not allow larger pasta shapes to cook completely.

2½ pounds cubed beef stew
    meat

¼ cup all-purpose flour

2 tablespoons olive oil

3 cups beef broth

16 baby carrots

8 fingerling potatoes,
   halved crosswise

1 medium onion, chopped

1 ounce dried oyster
  mushrooms, chopped

2 teaspoons garlic powder

1 teaspoon dried basil

1 teaspoon dried oregano

½ teaspoon dried
  rosemary

½ teaspoon dried
  marjoram

½ teaspoon dried sage

½ teaspoon dried thyme

   Salt and black pepper
   (optional)

   Chopped fresh Italian
   parsley (optional)

1 Combine beef and flour in large bowl; toss well to coat. Heat 1 tablespoon oil in large skillet over medium-high heat. Add half of beef; cook and stir 4 minutes or until browned. Remove to **CROCK-POT**® slow cooker. Repeat with remaining oil and beef.

2 Add broth, carrots, potatoes, onion, mushrooms, garlic powder, basil, oregano, rosemary, marjoram, sage and thyme to **CROCK-POT**® slow cooker; stir to blend. Cover; cook on LOW 10 to 12 hours or on HIGH 5 to 6 hours. Season with salt and pepper, if desired. Garnish with parsley.

MAKES 8 SERVINGS

DOUBLE THICK POTATO-CHEESE SOUP

2 pounds baking potatoes, cut into ½-inch cubes

2 cans (10½ ounces *each*) condensed cream of mushroom soup

1½ cups finely chopped green onions, divided

¼ teaspoon garlic powder

⅛ teaspoon ground red pepper

1½ cups (6 ounces) shredded sharp Cheddar cheese

1 cup (8 ounces) sour cream

1 cup milk

Black pepper

1 Combine potatoes, soup, 1 cup green onions, garlic powder and ground red pepper in **CROCK-POT®** slow cooker; stir to blend. Cover; cook on LOW 8 hours or on HIGH 4 hours.

2 Stir cheese, sour cream and milk into **CROCK-POT®** slow cooker until cheese is melted. Cover; cook on HIGH 10 minutes. Season with black pepper. Top each serving evenly with remaining ½ cup green onions.

MAKES 6 SERVINGS

CHICKEN AND MUSHROOM STEW

4 tablespoons vegetable oil, divided

2 medium leeks (white and light green parts only), halved lengthwise and thinly sliced crosswise

1 carrot, cut into 1-inch pieces

1 stalk celery, diced

6 boneless, skinless chicken thighs (about 2 pounds)

Salt and black pepper

12 ounces cremini mushrooms, quartered

1 ounce dried porcini mushrooms, rehydrated in 1½ cups hot water and chopped, soaking liquid strained and reserved

1 teaspoon minced garlic

1 sprig fresh thyme

1 whole bay leaf

¼ cup all-purpose flour

½ cup dry white wine

1 cup chicken broth

1 Heat 1 tablespoon oil in large skillet over medium heat. Add leeks; cook 8 minutes or until softened. Remove to **CROCK-POT**® slow cooker. Add carrot and celery.

2 Heat 1 tablespoon oil in same skillet over medium-high heat. Season chicken with salt and pepper. Add chicken in batches; cook 8 minutes or until browned on both sides. Remove to **CROCK-POT**® slow cooker.

3 Heat remaining 2 tablespoons oil in same skillet. Add cremini mushrooms; cook 7 minutes or until mushrooms have released their liquid and started to brown. Add porcini mushrooms, garlic, thyme, bay leaf and flour; cook and stir 1 minute. Add wine; cook and stir until evaporated, stirring to scrape up any browned bits from bottom of skillet. Add reserved soaking liquid and broth; bring to a simmer. Pour mixture into **CROCK-POT**® slow cooker.

4 Cover; cook on HIGH 2 to 3 hours. Remove thyme sprig and bay leaf before serving.

MAKES 6 SERVINGS

ROASTED TOMATO-BASIL SOUP

2 cans (28 ounces *each*) whole tomatoes, drained, 3 cups liquid reserved

2½ tablespoons packed dark brown sugar

1 medium onion, finely chopped

3 cups vegetable broth

3 tablespoons tomato paste

¼ teaspoon ground allspice

1 can (5 ounces) evaporated milk

¼ cup shredded fresh basil (about 10 large leaves)

Salt and black pepper

Sprigs fresh basil (optional)

1 Preheat oven to 450°F. Line baking sheet with foil; spray with nonstick cooking spray. Arrange tomatoes on foil in single layer. Sprinkle with brown sugar; top with onion. Bake 25 minutes or until tomatoes look dry and light brown. Let tomatoes cool slightly; finely chop.

2 Place tomato mixture, 3 cups reserved liquid from tomatoes, broth, tomato paste and allspice in **CROCK-POT**® slow cooker; mix well. Cover; cook on LOW 8 hours or on HIGH 4 hours.

3 Add evaporated milk and shredded basil; season with salt and pepper. Cover; cook on HIGH 30 minutes or until heated through. Garnish each serving with basil sprigs.

MAKES 6 SERVINGS

HEARTY CHICKEN NOODLE SOUP

1¼ pounds boneless, skinless chicken breasts, cut into 1-inch pieces

1¼ pounds boneless, skinless chicken thighs

4 cans (about 14 ounces *each*) chicken broth

12 baby carrots, cut into ½-inch pieces

4 stalks celery, cut into ½-inch pieces

¾ cup finely chopped onion

4 cubes chicken bouillon

1 teaspoon dried Italian parsley flakes

½ teaspoon black pepper

¼ teaspoon ground red pepper

1 teaspoon salt

2 cups uncooked egg noodles

1 Place chicken in **CROCK-POT**® slow cooker. Add broth, carrots, celery, onion, bouillon cubes, parsley flakes, black pepper, ground red pepper and salt. Cover; cook on LOW 5 to 6 hours.

2 Stir in egg noodles. Turn **CROCK-POT**® slow cooker to HIGH. Cover; cook on HIGH 30 minutes or until noodles are tender.

MAKES 8 TO 10 SERVINGS

THREE-BEAN CHILI WITH CHORIZO

2 Mexican chorizo sausages (about 6 ounces *each*), casings removed

1 tablespoon vegetable oil

1 large onion, chopped

1 tablespoon salt

1 tablespoon tomato paste

1 tablespoon minced garlic

1 tablespoon chili powder

1 tablespoon ancho chili powder

2 to 3 teaspoons chipotle chili powder

2 teaspoons ground cumin

1 teaspoon ground coriander

3 cups water

2 cans (about 14 ounces *each*) crushed tomatoes

½ cup dried pinto beans, rinsed and sorted

½ cup dried kidney beans, rinsed and sorted

½ cup dried black beans, rinsed and sorted

Chopped fresh cilantro (optional)

1 Heat large nonstick skillet over medium-high heat. Add sausages; cook 3 to 4 minutes, stirring to break up meat. Remove to **CROCK-POT**® slow cooker using slotted spoon.

2 Wipe out skillet. Heat oil in same skillet over medium heat. Add onion; cook and stir 6 minutes or until softened. Add salt, tomato paste, garlic, chili powders, cumin and coriander; cook and stir 1 minute. Remove to **CROCK-POT**® slow cooker. Stir in water, tomatoes and beans.

3 Cover; cook on LOW 10 hours. Garnish each serving with cilantro.

MAKES 6 TO 8 SERVINGS

NOTE: For a spicier chili, increase the chipotle chili powder to 1 tablespoon.

HEARTY CHICKEN TEQUILA SOUP

1 **small onion, cut into 8 wedges**

1 **cup frozen corn**

1 **can (about 14 ounces) diced tomatoes with mild green chiles**

2 **cloves garlic, minced**

2 **tablespoons chopped fresh cilantro, plus additional for garnish**

1 **whole fryer chicken (about 3½ pounds)**

2 **cups chicken broth**

3 **tablespoons tequila**

¼ **cup sour cream**

1 Place onion wedges on bottom of **CROCK-POT®** slow cooker. Add corn, tomatoes, garlic and 2 tablespoons cilantro; stir to blend. Place chicken on top of tomato mixture.

2 Pour broth and tequila over chicken and tomato mixture. Cover; cook on LOW 8 to 10 hours.

3 Remove chicken to large cutting board; discard skin and bones. Shred chicken with two forks. Stir shredded chicken into **CROCK-POT®** slow cooker. Top each serving with a dollop of sour cream and garnish with additional cilantro.

MAKES 2 TO 4 SERVINGS

THREE-BEAN MOLE CHILI

1 can (about 15 ounces) chili beans in spicy sauce, undrained

1 can (about 15 ounces) pinto beans, rinsed and drained

1 can (about 15 ounces) black beans, rinsed and drained

1 can (about 14 ounces) Mexican or chili-style diced tomatoes

1 large green bell pepper, chopped

1 small onion, chopped

½ cup vegetable broth

¼ cup prepared mole paste*

2 teaspoons minced garlic

2 teaspoons ground cumin

2 teaspoons chili powder

2 teaspoons ground coriander (optional)

Optional toppings: crushed tortilla chips, sprigs fresh cilantro, shredded Cheddar cheese

*Mole paste is available in the Mexican section of large supermarkets and at specialty markets.

Combine beans, tomatoes, bell pepper, onion, broth, mole paste, garlic, cumin, chili powder and coriander, if desired, in **CROCK-POT**® slow cooker; stir to blend. Cover; cook on LOW 5 to 6 hours. Serve with desired toppings.

MAKES 4 TO 6 SERVINGS

TIP: Opening the lid and checking on food in the **CROCK-POT**® slow cooker can affect both cooking time and results. Due to the nature of slow cooking, there's no need to stir the food unless the recipe method says to do so.

WILD MUSHROOM BEEF STEW

1½ to 2 pounds cubed beef stew meat

2 tablespoons all-purpose flour

½ teaspoon salt

½ teaspoon black pepper

1½ cups beef broth

4 shiitake mushrooms, sliced

2 medium carrots, sliced

2 medium potatoes, diced

1 small white onion, chopped

1 stalk celery, sliced

1 teaspoon paprika

1 clove garlic, minced

1 teaspoon Worcestershire sauce

1 whole bay leaf

Place beef in **CROCK-POT**® slow cooker. Combine flour, salt and pepper in small bowl; stir to blend. Sprinkle flour mixture over meat; toss to coat. Add broth, mushrooms, carrots, potatoes, onion, celery, paprika, garlic, Worcestershire sauce and bay leaf; stir to blend. Cover; cook on LOW 10 to 12 hours or on HIGH 4 to 6 hours. Remove and discard bay leaf.

MAKES 5 SERVINGS

NOTE: If shiitake mushrooms are unavailable in your local grocery store, you can substitute other mushrooms of your choice. For extra punch, add a few dried porcini mushrooms.

TIP: You may double the amount of meat, mushrooms, carrots, potatoes, onion and celery for a 5-, 6- or 7-quart **CROCK-POT**® slow cooker.

BLACK AND WHITE CHILI

Nonstick cooking spray

1 pound boneless, skinless chicken breasts, cut into ¾-inch pieces

1 cup chopped onion

1 can (about 15 ounces) Great Northern beans, rinsed and drained

1 can (about 15 ounces) black beans, rinsed and drained

1 can (about 14 ounces) stewed tomatoes

2 tablespoons Texas-style chili seasoning mix

1 Spray large skillet with cooking spray; heat over medium heat. Add chicken and onion; cook and stir 5 minutes or until chicken is browned.

2 Combine chicken mixture, beans, tomatoes and chili seasoning mix in **CROCK-POT**® slow cooker; stir to blend. Cover; cook on LOW 4 to 4½ hours.

MAKES 6 SERVINGS

SERVING SUGGESTION: For a change of pace, this delicious chili is excellent served over cooked rice or pasta.

NANA'S MINI MEATBALL SOUP

1 pound ground beef

1 pound ground pork

1½ cups finely grated Pecorino Romano or Parmesan cheese

1 cup seasoned dry bread crumbs

2 eggs

1 bunch fresh Italian parsley

Salt and black pepper

3 quarts chicken broth

1 bunch escarole, coarsely chopped*

½ (16-ounce) package ditalini pasta, cooked and drained

*You may substitute spinach.

1 Combine beef, pork, cheese, bread crumbs, eggs, parsley, salt and pepper in large bowl until well blended. Shape into ¾-inch meatballs.

2 Add meatballs and broth to **CROCK-POT**® slow cooker. Cover; cook on LOW 9 hours or on HIGH 5 hours.

3 Add escarole. Cover; cook on LOW 15 minutes or until wilted. Stir in pasta just before serving.

MAKES 6 TO 8 SERVINGS

LAMB AND CHICKPEA STEW

1 pound lamb stew meat

2 teaspoons salt, divided

2 tablespoons vegetable oil, divided

1 large onion, chopped

1 tablespoon minced garlic

1½ teaspoons ground cumin

1 teaspoon ground turmeric

1 teaspoon ground coriander

1 teaspoon ground cinnamon

¼ teaspoon black pepper

2 cups chicken broth

1 cup diced canned tomatoes, drained

1 cup dried chickpeas, rinsed and sorted

½ cup chopped dried apricots

¼ cup chopped fresh Italian parsley

2 tablespoons honey

2 tablespoons lemon juice

Hot cooked couscous

1 Season lamb with 1 teaspoon salt. Heat 1 tablespoon oil in large skillet over medium-high heat. Add lamb; cook and stir 8 minutes or until browned on all sides. Remove to **CROCK-POT**® slow cooker.

2 Heat remaining 1 tablespoon oil in same skillet over medium heat. Add onion; cook and stir 6 minutes or until softened. Add garlic, remaining 1 teaspoon salt, cumin, turmeric, coriander, cinnamon and pepper; cook and stir 1 minute. Add broth and tomatoes; cook and stir 5 minutes, scraping up any brown bits from bottom of skillet. Remove to **CROCK-POT**® slow cooker. Stir in chickpeas.

3 Cover; cook on LOW 7 hours. Stir in apricots. Cover; cook on LOW 1 hour. Turn off heat. Let stand 10 minutes. Skim off and discard fat. Stir in parsley, honey and lemon juice. Serve over couscous.

MAKES 6 SERVINGS

CLASSIC CHILI

1½ pounds ground beef

1½ cups chopped onion

1 cup chopped green bell pepper

2 cloves garlic, minced

3 cans (about 15 ounces *each*) dark red kidney beans, rinsed and drained

2 cans (about 15 ounces *each*) tomato sauce

1 can (about 14 ounces) diced tomatoes

2 to 3 teaspoons chili powder

1 to 2 teaspoons ground mustard

¾ teaspoon dried basil

½ teaspoon black pepper

1 to 2 dried red chiles (optional)

Shredded Cheddar cheese (optional)

Sprigs fresh cilantro (optional)

1 Brown beef, onion, bell pepper and garlic in large skillet over medium-high heat 6 to 8 minutes, stirring to break up meat. Remove beef mixture to **CROCK-POT**® slow cooker using slotted spoon.

2 Add beans, tomato sauce, tomatoes, chili powder, mustard, basil, black pepper and chiles, if desired, to **CROCK-POT**® slow cooker; stir to blend. Cover; cook on LOW 8 to 10 hours or on HIGH 4 to 5 hours. If used, remove chiles before serving. Top with cheese, if desired. Garnish with cilantro.

MAKES 6 SERVINGS

ITALIAN HILLSIDE GARDEN SOUP

1 tablespoon olive oil

1 cup chopped green bell pepper

1 cup chopped onion

½ cup sliced celery

1 can (about 14 ounces) diced tomatoes with basil, garlic and oregano

1 can (about 15 ounces) navy beans, rinsed and drained

1 medium zucchini, chopped

1 cup frozen cut green beans

2 cans (about 14 ounces *each*) chicken broth

¼ teaspoon garlic powder

1 package (9 ounces) refrigerated sausage- or cheese-filled tortellini pasta

3 tablespoons chopped fresh basil

Grated Asiago or Parmesan cheese (optional)

1 Heat oil in large skillet over medium-high heat. Add bell pepper, onion and celery; cook and stir 4 minutes or until onion is translucent. Remove to **CROCK-POT**® slow cooker.

2 Add tomatoes, navy beans, zucchini, green beans, broth and garlic powder. Cover; cook on LOW 7 hours or on HIGH 3½ hours.

3 Add tortellini. Cover; cook on HIGH 20 to 25 minutes or until pasta is tender. Stir in basil. Garnish with cheese.

MAKES 6 SERVINGS

TIP: Cooking times are guidelines. **CROCK-POT**® slow cookers, just like ovens, cook differently depending on a variety of factors, including capacity and altitude.

HEARTY PORK AND BACON CHILI

2½ pounds pork shoulder, cut into 1-inch pieces

3½ teaspoons salt, divided

1¼ teaspoons black pepper, divided

1 tablespoon vegetable oil

4 slices thick-cut bacon, diced

2 medium onions, chopped

1 red bell pepper, chopped

¼ cup chili powder

2 tablespoons tomato paste

1 tablespoon minced garlic

1 tablespoon ground cumin

1 tablespoon smoked paprika

1 bottle (12 ounces) pale ale

2 cans (about 14 ounces *each*) diced tomatoes

2 cups water

¾ cup dried kidney beans, rinsed and sorted

¾ cup dried black beans, rinsed and sorted

3 tablespoons cornmeal

Feta cheese and chopped fresh cilantro (optional)

1 Season pork with 1 teaspoon salt and 1 teaspoon black pepper. Heat oil in large skillet over medium-high heat. Cook pork in batches 6 minutes or until browned on all sides. Remove to **CROCK-POT**® slow cooker using slotted spoon.

2 Heat same skillet over medium heat. Add bacon; cook and stir until crisp. Remove to **CROCK-POT**® slow cooker using slotted spoon.

3 Pour off all but 2 tablespoons fat from skillet. Return skillet to medium heat. Add onions and bell pepper; cook and stir 6 minutes or just until softened. Stir in chili powder, tomato paste, garlic, cumin, paprika, remaining 2½ teaspoons salt and remaining ¼ teaspoon black pepper; cook and stir 1 minute. Stir in ale. Bring to a simmer, scraping up any browned bits from the bottom of skillet. Pour over pork in **CROCK-POT**® slow cooker. Stir in tomatoes, water, beans and cornmeal.

4 Cover; cook on LOW 10 hours. Turn off heat. Let stand 10 minutes. Skim fat from surface. Garnish each serving with cheese and cilantro.

MAKES 8 TO 10 SERVINGS

FRENCH ONION SOUP

¼ cup (½ stick) butter

3 pounds yellow onions, sliced

1 tablespoon sugar

2 to 3 tablespoons dry white wine or water (optional)

8 cups beef broth

8 to 16 slices French bread (optional)

½ cup (2 ounces) shredded Gruyère or Swiss cheese

1 Melt butter in large skillet over medium-low heat. Add onions; cover and cook 10 minutes or just until onions are tender and transparent, but not browned.

2 Remove cover. Sprinkle sugar over onions; cook and stir 8 to 10 minutes or until onions are caramelized. Add onions and any browned bits to **CROCK-POT**® slow cooker. Add wine, if desired, to skillet. Bring to a boil, scraping up any browned bits. Add to **CROCK-POT**® slow cooker. Stir in broth. Cover; cook on LOW 8 hours or on HIGH 6 hours.

3 Preheat broiler. To serve, ladle soup into individual soup bowls. If desired, top each with 1 or 2 bread slices and about 1 tablespoon cheese. Place under broiler until cheese is melted and bubbly.

MAKES 8 SERVINGS

VARIATION: Substitute 1 cup dry white wine for 1 cup of beef broth.

LEEK AND POTATO SOUP

6 slices bacon, crisp-cooked, chopped and divided

5 cups shredded frozen hash brown potatoes

3 leeks (white and light green parts only), cut into ¾-inch pieces

1 can (about 14 ounces) vegetable broth

1 can (10¾ ounces) condensed cream of potato soup, undiluted

2 stalks celery, sliced

1 can (5 ounces) evaporated milk

½ cup sour cream

Set aside 2 tablespoons bacon. Combine remaining bacon, potatoes, leeks, broth, soup, celery and evaporated milk in **CROCK-POT**® slow cooker. Cover; cook on LOW 6 to 7 hours. Stir in sour cream. Sprinkle each serving with reserved bacon.

MAKES 4 TO 6 SERVINGS

CHICKEN STEW WITH HERB DUMPLINGS

2 cups sliced carrots

1 cup chopped onion

1 green bell pepper, sliced

½ cup sliced celery

2 cans (about 14 ounces *each*) chicken broth, divided

⅔ cup all-purpose flour

1 pound boneless, skinless chicken breasts, cut into 1-inch pieces

1 large red potato, unpeeled and cut into 1-inch pieces

6 ounces mushrooms, halved

¾ cup frozen peas

1¼ teaspoons dried basil, divided

1 teaspoon dried rosemary, divided

½ teaspoon dried tarragon, divided

¼ cup whipping cream

¾ to 1 teaspoon salt

¼ teaspoon black pepper

1 cup biscuit baking mix

⅓ cup milk

1 Combine carrots, onion, bell pepper, celery and all but 1 cup broth in **CROCK-POT**® slow cooker. Cover; cook on LOW 2 hours.

2 Stir remaining 1 cup broth into flour in small bowl until smooth. Stir into vegetable mixture. Add chicken, potato, mushrooms, peas, 1 teaspoon basil, ¾ teaspoon rosemary and ¼ teaspoon tarragon. Cover; cook on LOW 4 hours or until vegetables and chicken are tender. Stir in cream, salt and black pepper.

3 Combine baking mix, remaining ¼ teaspoon basil, ¼ teaspoon rosemary and ¼ teaspoon tarragon in small bowl. Stir in milk until soft dough forms. Add dumpling mixture to top of stew in four large spoonfuls.

4 Cook, uncovered, on LOW 30 minutes. Cover; cook on LOW 30 to 45 minutes or until dumplings are firm and toothpick inserted into center comes out clean. Serve in shallow bowls.

MAKES 4 SERVINGS

CAJUN PORK SAUSAGE AND SHRIMP STEW

1 can (28 ounces) diced tomatoes

1 package (16 ounces) frozen mixed vegetables (potatoes, carrots, celery and onions)

1 package (14 to 16 ounces) kielbasa or smoked sausage, cut diagonally into ¾-inch slices

2 teaspoons Cajun seasoning

¾ pound large raw shrimp, peeled and deveined (with tails on)

2 cups (8 ounces) frozen sliced okra, thawed

Hot cooked rice or grits

1 Coat inside of **CROCK-POT**® slow cooker with nonstick cooking spray. Combine tomatoes, vegetables, sausage and Cajun seasoning in **CROCK-POT**® slow cooker; stir to blend. Cover; cook on LOW 5 to 6 hours or on HIGH 2 to 2½ hours.

2 Stir shrimp and okra into **CROCK-POT**® slow cooker. Cover; cook on HIGH 30 to 35 minutes or until shrimp are opaque. Serve over rice.

MAKES 6 SERVINGS

CHICKEN DINNERS

CHICKEN VESUVIO

3 tablespoons all-purpose flour

1½ teaspoons dried oregano

1 teaspoon salt

½ teaspoon black pepper

1 frying chicken, cut up and trimmed *or* 3 pounds bone-in chicken pieces, trimmed

2 tablespoons olive oil

4 small baking potatoes, unpeeled and cut into 8 wedges *each*

2 small onions, cut into thin wedges

4 cloves garlic, minced

¼ cup chicken broth

¼ cup dry white wine

¼ cup chopped fresh Italian parsley

1 Combine flour, oregano, salt and pepper in large resealable food storage bag. Add chicken, several pieces at a time, to bag; shake to coat lightly with flour mixture. Heat oil in large skillet over medium heat. Add chicken; cook 10 to 12 minutes or until browned on all sides.

2 Place potatoes, onions and garlic in **CROCK-POT**® slow cooker. Add broth and wine; top with chicken pieces. Pour pan juices from skillet over chicken. Cover; cook on LOW 6 to 7 hours or on HIGH 3 to 3½ hours.

3 Remove chicken and vegetables to serving plates; top with juices from **CROCK-POT**® slow cooker. Sprinkle with parsley.

MAKES 4 TO 6 SERVINGS

8 ounces mushrooms, sliced

1 medium onion, cut into thin wedges

1 tablespoon olive oil

4 boneless, skinless chicken breasts

1 jar (24 to 26 ounces) pasta sauce

½ teaspoon dried basil

¼ teaspoon dried oregano

1 whole bay leaf

½ cup (2 ounces) shredded mozzarella cheese

¼ cup grated Parmesan cheese

Hot cooked spaghetti

Chopped fresh basil (optional)

1 Place mushrooms and onion in **CROCK-POT**® slow cooker.

2 Heat oil in large skillet over medium-high heat. Add chicken; cook 5 to 6 minutes on each side or until browned. Place chicken in **CROCK-POT**® slow cooker. Pour pasta sauce over chicken; add dried basil, oregano and bay leaf. Cover; cook on LOW 6 to 7 hours or on HIGH 3 to 4 hours. Remove and discard bay leaf.

3 Sprinkle chicken with cheeses. Cook, uncovered, on LOW 10 minutes or until cheeses are melted. Serve over spaghetti and garnish with fresh basil.

MAKES 4 SERVINGS

TIP: Dairy products should be added at the end of the cooking time because they will curdle if cooked in the **CROCK-POT**® slow cooker for a long time.

CHICKEN CORDON BLEU

¼ cup all-purpose flour

1 teaspoon paprika

½ teaspoon salt

¼ teaspoon black pepper

4 boneless chicken breasts, lightly pounded*

4 slices ham

4 slices Swiss cheese

2 tablespoons olive oil

½ cup dry white wine

½ cup chicken broth

½ cup half-and-half

2 tablespoons cornstarch

*Place chicken between two pieces of plastic wrap and flatten with meat mallet or back of skillet.

1 Combine flour, paprika, salt and pepper in large resealable food storage bag.

2 Place flattened chicken on large cutting board, skin side down. Place 1 slice ham and 1 slice cheese on each piece. Fold chicken up to enclose filling; secure with toothpick. Place in bag with seasoned flour; shake gently to coat.

3 Heat oil in large skillet over medium-high heat. Brown chicken on all sides. Remove to **CROCK-POT**® slow cooker.

4 Remove skillet from heat; add wine, stirring to scrape up browned bits. Pour into **CROCK-POT**® slow cooker. Add broth. Cover; cook on LOW 2 hours.

5 Remove chicken with slotted spoon. Cover and keep warm. Stir half-and-half into cornstarch in small bowl until smooth. Stir into cooking liquid. Cover; cook on LOW 15 minutes or until thickened. Remove and discard toothpicks. Serve chicken with cooking liquid.

MAKES 4 SERVINGS

CHICKEN SCALOPPINE IN ALFREDO SAUCE

2 tablespoons all-purpose flour

¼ teaspoon salt

¼ teaspoon black pepper

6 pounds boneless, skinless chicken tenderloins (about 1 pound), cut lengthwise in half

1 tablespoon butter

1 tablespoon olive oil

1 cup Alfredo pasta sauce

1 package (12 ounces) uncooked spinach noodles

1 Place flour, salt and pepper in large bowl; stir to combine. Add chicken; toss to coat. Heat butter and oil in large skillet over medium-high heat. Add chicken; cook 3 minutes per side or until browned. Remove chicken in single layer to **CROCK-POT**® slow cooker.

2 Add Alfredo pasta sauce to **CROCK-POT**® slow cooker. Cover; cook on LOW 1 to 1½ hours.

3 Meanwhile, cook noodles according to package directions. Drain; place in large shallow bowl. Spoon chicken and sauce over noodles.

MAKES 6 SERVINGS

SPANISH CHICKEN WITH RICE

2 tablespoons olive oil

11 ounces cooked linguiça or kielbasa sausage, sliced into ½-inch rounds

6 boneless, skinless chicken thighs (about 1 pound)

1 onion, chopped

5 cloves garlic, minced

2 cups uncooked converted long grain rice

½ cup diced carrots

1 red bell pepper, chopped

½ teaspoon salt

¼ teaspoon black pepper

¼ teaspoon saffron threads (optional)

3½ cups hot chicken broth

½ cup peas

1 Heat oil in medium skillet over medium heat. Add sausage; cook and stir until browned. Remove to **CROCK-POT®** slow cooker using slotted spoon.

2 Add chicken to skillet; brown on all sides. Remove to **CROCK-POT®** slow cooker. Add onion to skillet; cook and stir 5 minutes or until soft. Stir in garlic; cook 30 seconds. Remove to **CROCK-POT®** slow cooker.

3 Add rice, carrots, bell pepper, salt, black pepper and saffron, if desired, to **CROCK-POT®** slow cooker. Pour broth over mixture. Cover; cook on HIGH 3½ to 4 hours.

4 Stir in peas. Cover; cook on HIGH 15 minutes or until heated through.

MAKES 6 SERVINGS

6 skinless chicken thighs (about 2 pounds)

¼ teaspoon salt, plus additional for seasoning

¼ teaspoon black pepper, plus additional for seasoning

1 tablespoon vegetable oil

1 large onion, chopped

2 cloves garlic, minced

2 tablespoons grated fresh ginger

½ teaspoon ground cinnamon

⅛ teaspoon ground allspice

1 can (about 14 ounces) diced tomatoes

1 cup chicken broth

1 package (8 ounces) dried apricots

Pinch saffron threads (optional)

Hot cooked basmati rice

2 tablespoons chopped fresh Italian parsley (optional)

1 Coat inside of **CROCK-POT®** slow cooker with nonstick cooking spray. Season chicken with ¼ teaspoon salt and ¼ teaspoon pepper. Heat oil in large skillet over medium-high heat. Brown chicken on all sides. Remove to **CROCK-POT®** slow cooker.

2 Add onion to skillet; cook and stir 3 to 5 minutes or until translucent. Stir in garlic, ginger, cinnamon and allspice; cook and stir 15 to 30 seconds or until mixture is fragrant. Add tomatoes and broth; cook 2 to 3 minutes or until mixture is heated through. Pour into **CROCK-POT®** slow cooker.

3 Add apricots and saffron, if desired. Cover; cook on LOW 5 to 6 hours or on HIGH 3 to 4 hours. Season with additional salt and pepper, if desired. Serve with basmati rice and garnish with parsley.

MAKES 4 TO 6 SERVINGS

NOTE: To skin chicken easily, grasp skin with paper towel and pull away. Repeat with fresh paper towel for each piece of chicken, discarding skins and towels.

CHICKEN FAJITAS WITH BARBECUE SAUCE

- 1 can (8 ounces) tomato sauce
- ⅓ cup chopped green onions
- ¼ cup ketchup
- 2 tablespoons water
- 2 tablespoons orange juice
- 2 cloves garlic, finely chopped
- 1 tablespoon cider vinegar
- 1 tablespoon chili sauce
- ½ teaspoon vegetable oil
  Dash Worcestershire sauce
  Nonstick cooking spray
- 10 ounces boneless, skinless chicken breasts, cut into ½-inch strips
- 2 green or red bell peppers, thinly sliced
- 1 cup sliced onion
- 2 cups tomato wedges
- 4 (6-inch) flour tortillas, heated

1 Combine tomato sauce, green onions, ketchup, water, orange juice, garlic, vinegar, chili sauce, oil and Worcestershire sauce in **CROCK-POT®** slow cooker; stir to blend. Cover; cook on HIGH 1½ hours.

2 Spray large skillet with cooking spray; heat over medium heat. Add chicken; cook and stir 5 to 7 minutes.

3 Turn **CROCK-POT®** slow cooker to LOW. Add chicken, bell peppers and sliced onion to **CROCK-POT®** slow cooker; stir to blend. Cover; cook on LOW 3 to 4 hours.

4 Add tomato wedges to **CROCK-POT®** slow cooker. Cover; cook on LOW 30 to 45 minutes or until heated through. Serve with tortillas.

MAKES 4 SERVINGS

THREE ONION CHICKEN

3 tablespoons butter

3 onions, chopped

3 leeks (white and light
   green parts only),
   sliced

2 cloves garlic, chopped

½ cup dry white wine

2 tablespoons lemon juice

½ cup chicken broth

6 boneless, skinless
   chicken breasts
   (6 ounces *each*)

1 teaspoon salt

¼ teaspoon black pepper

½ teaspoon dried thyme

2 green onions, sliced

1 Melt butter in large skillet over medium-high heat. Add onions; cook and stir 3 to 5 minutes or until translucent. Add leeks; cook and stir 5 minutes or until onions are golden brown and leeks are tender. Add garlic; cook and stir 30 seconds. Add wine and lemon juice; cook and stir until most liquid is evaporated. Remove to **CROCK-POT**® slow cooker. Pour in broth.

2 Sprinkle chicken with salt and pepper. Add chicken to **CROCK-POT**® slow cooker. Sprinkle with thyme. Cover; cook on HIGH 1½ hours or until chicken is cooked through. Sprinkle with green onions before serving.

MAKES 6 SERVINGS

CHICKEN MARBELLA

10 boneless, skinless
   chicken breasts
   (6 ounces *each*)

1 teaspoon salt

¼ teaspoon black pepper

2 tablespoons olive oil

¾ cup dry white wine

½ cup balsamic vinegar

12 cloves garlic, crushed

1 cup dried figs or prunes,
   halved lengthwise

¾ cup packed brown sugar

½ cup black olives

1 jar (3½ ounces) capers,
   drained and juice
   reserved

6 whole bay leaves

1 teaspoon dried oregano

1 tablespoon plus
   1½ teaspoons
   cornstarch

1 Season chicken with salt and pepper. Heat oil in large skillet over medium-high heat. Cook chicken in batches 4 to 5 minutes or until browned on both sides. Place chicken in **CROCK-POT®** slow cooker. Add wine and vinegar to skillet, scraping up any browned bits. Pour over chicken.

2 Add garlic, figs, brown sugar, olives, capers, 2 teaspoons reserved caper juice and bay leaves to **CROCK-POT®** slow cooker. Cover; cook on LOW 3 to 4 hours or on HIGH 1½ to 2 hours.

3 Remove chicken to large serving plate; keep warm. Strain cooking liquid through sieve into large bowl. Remove and discard bay leaves; reserve figs, olives and capers. Return liquid to **CROCK-POT®** slow cooker. Stir oregano into liquid. Whisk ¼ cup liquid into cornstarch in small bowl until smooth. Whisk into cooking liquid in **CROCK-POT®** slow cooker. Cook, uncovered, on HIGH 10 to 15 minutes or until thickened.

4 Serve chicken with reserved figs, olives and capers. Top with sauce.

MAKES 10 SERVINGS

NOTE: Chicken Marbella is known for its distinctive flavors of prunes, olives and capers.

BEER CHICKEN

2 tablespoons olive oil

1 cut-up whole chicken
    (3 to 5 pounds)

10 new potatoes, halved

1 can (12 ounces) beer

2 medium carrots, thinly
    sliced

1 cup chopped celery

1 medium onion, chopped

1 tablespoon chopped
    fresh rosemary

1 Heat oil in large skillet over medium heat. Add chicken; cook 5 to 7 minutes on each side or until browned. Remove to **CROCK-POT**® slow cooker.

2 Add potatoes, beer, carrots, celery, onion and rosemary to **CROCK-POT**® slow cooker. Cover; cook on HIGH 5 hours.

MAKES 4 TO 6 SERVINGS

MIXED HERB AND BUTTER RUBBED CHICKEN

3 tablespoons butter, softened

1 tablespoon grated lemon peel

2 teaspoons chopped fresh rosemary

1 teaspoon chopped fresh thyme

¾ teaspoon salt

¼ teaspoon black pepper

1 whole chicken (4½ to 5 pounds)

1 Coat inside of **CROCK-POT**® slow cooker with nonstick cooking spray. Combine butter, lemon peel, rosemary, thyme, salt and pepper in small bowl; stir to blend. Loosen skin over breast meat and drumsticks; pat chicken dry with paper towels. Rub butter mixture over and under the chicken skin. Place chicken in **CROCK-POT**® slow cooker.

2 Cover; cook on LOW 5 to 6 hours, basting every 30 minutes with cooking liquid. Remove chicken to large cutting board. Let stand 15 minutes before cutting into pieces.

MAKES 4 TO 6 SERVINGS

BASQUE CHICKEN WITH PEPPERS

1 cut-up whole chicken
  (4 pounds)

2 teaspoons salt, divided

1 teaspoon black pepper,
  divided

1½ tablespoons olive oil

1 onion, chopped

1 medium green bell
  pepper, cut into strips

1 medium yellow bell
  pepper, cut into strips

1 medium red bell pepper,
  cut into strips

8 ounces small brown
  mushrooms, halved

1 can (about 14 ounces)
  stewed tomatoes,
  undrained

½ cup chicken broth

½ cup Rioja wine

3 ounces tomato paste

2 cloves garlic, minced

1 sprig fresh marjoram

1 teaspoon smoked paprika

  Hot cooked rice pilaf

4 ounces chopped
  prosciutto

1 Season chicken with 1 teaspoon salt and ½ teaspoon black pepper. Heat oil in large skillet over medium-high heat. Add chicken in batches; cook 6 to 8 minutes or until browned on all sides. Remove to **CROCK-POT**® slow cooker.

2 Reduce skillet heat to medium-low. Add onion; cook and stir 3 minutes or until softened. Add bell peppers and mushrooms; cook 3 minutes. Add tomatoes, broth, wine, tomato paste, garlic, marjoram, remaining 1 teaspoon salt, paprika and remaining ½ teaspoon black pepper to skillet; bring to a simmer. Simmer 3 to 4 minutes; pour over chicken in **CROCK-POT**® slow cooker. Cover; cook on LOW 5 to 6 hours or on HIGH 4 hours.

3 Serve chicken over rice. Ladle vegetables and sauce over chicken. Sprinkle with prosciutto.

MAKES 4 TO 6 SERVINGS

PINEAPPLE AND BUTTERNUT SQUASH BRAISED CHICKEN

- 1 medium butternut squash, cut into 1-inch pieces (about 3 cups)
- 1 can (20 ounces) pineapple chunks, undrained
- ½ cup ketchup
- 2 tablespoons packed brown sugar
- 8 chicken thighs (about 2 pounds)
- ½ teaspoon salt
- ¼ teaspoon black pepper

1 Coat inside of **CROCK-POT®** slow cooker with nonstick cooking spray. Combine squash, pineapple with juice, ketchup and brown sugar in **CROCK-POT®** slow cooker; stir to blend. Season chicken with salt and pepper. Place chicken on top of squash mixture.

2 Cover; cook on LOW 5 to 6 hours. Remove chicken to large platter; cover loosely with foil. Turn **CROCK-POT®** slow cooker to HIGH. Cook, uncovered, on HIGH 10 to 15 minutes or until sauce is thickened. Serve sauce over chicken.

MAKES 4 SERVINGS

SHREDDED CHICKEN TACOS

2 pounds boneless, skinless chicken thighs

½ cup prepared mango salsa, plus additional for serving

8 (6-inch) yellow corn tortillas, warmed

Lettuce (optional)

1 Coat inside of **CROCK-POT**® slow cooker with nonstick cooking spray. Add chicken and ½ cup salsa. Cover; cook on LOW 4 to 5 hours or on HIGH 2½ to 3 hours.

2 Remove chicken to large cutting board; shred with two forks. Stir shredded chicken back into **CROCK-POT**® slow cooker. To serve, divide chicken and lettuce, if desired, evenly among tortillas. Serve with additional salsa.

MAKES 4 SERVINGS

BASIL CHICKEN MERLOT WITH WILD MUSHROOMS

3 tablespoons extra virgin olive oil, divided

1 roasting chicken (about 3 pounds), skinned and cut up

1½ cups thickly sliced cremini mushrooms

1 medium yellow onion, diced

2 cloves garlic, minced

1 cup chicken broth

1 can (6 ounces) tomato paste

⅓ cup Merlot or dry red wine

2 teaspoons sugar

1 teaspoon ground oregano

¼ teaspoon salt

¼ teaspoon black pepper

2 tablespoons minced fresh basil

3 cups hot cooked ziti pasta, drained

1 Heat 1½ to 2 tablespoons oil in skillet over medium heat. Working in batches, brown chicken pieces on each side 3 to 5 minutes, turning once. Remove to plate with slotted spoon.

2 Heat remaining oil in skillet. Add mushrooms, onion and garlic; cook and stir 7 to 8 minutes or until onion is soft. Remove to **CROCK-POT®** slow cooker. Top with chicken.

3 Combine broth, tomato paste, wine, sugar, oregano, salt and pepper in medium bowl. Pour sauce over chicken. Cover; cook on LOW 7 to 9 hours or on HIGH 3 to 4 hours.

4 Stir in basil. Place pasta in serving bowls. Ladle chicken, mushrooms and sauce evenly over pasta.

MAKES 4 TO 6 SERVINGS

CHICKEN AND BISCUITS

4 boneless, skinless chicken breasts, cut into 1-inch pieces

1 can (10¾ ounces) condensed cream of chicken soup

1 package (10 ounces) frozen peas and carrots

1 package (7½ ounces) refrigerated biscuits

1 Place chicken in **CROCK-POT**® slow cooker; pour in soup. Cover; cook on LOW 4 hours.

2 Stir in peas and carrots. Cover; cook on LOW 30 minutes or until vegetables are heated through.

3 Meanwhile, bake biscuits according to package directions. Spoon chicken and vegetable mixture over biscuits to serve.

MAKES 4 SERVINGS

CHICKEN AND DRESSING

4 boneless, skinless chicken breasts (about 1 pound)

Salt and black pepper

4 slices Swiss cheese

2 cans (10¾ ounces *each*) condensed cream of chicken, celery or mushroom soup, undiluted

1 can (about 14 ounces) chicken broth

3 cups packaged stuffing mix

½ cup (1 stick) butter, melted

Place chicken in **CROCK-POT®** slow cooker. Season with salt and pepper. Top each breast with cheese slice. Add soup and broth. Sprinkle stuffing mix over top; pour melted butter over all in **CROCK-POT®** slow cooker. Cover; cook on LOW 6 to 8 hours or on HIGH 3 to 4 hours.

MAKES 4 SERVINGS

CHICKEN PARMESAN WITH EGGPLANT

6 boneless, skinless chicken breasts

2 eggs

2 teaspoons salt

2 teaspoons black pepper

2 cups seasoned dry bread crumbs

½ cup olive oil

½ cup (1 stick) butter

2 small eggplants, cut into ¾-inch-thick slices

1½ cups grated Parmesan cheese

2¼ cups tomato-basil pasta sauce

1 pound sliced or shredded mozzarella cheese

1 Slice chicken breasts in half lengthwise. Cut each half lengthwise again to get four ¾-inch slices.

2 Combine eggs, salt and pepper in medium bowl; whisk to blend. Place bread crumbs in separate medium bowl. Dip chicken in egg mixture; turn to coat. Then coat chicken with bread crumbs, covering both sides evenly.

3 Heat oil and butter in large skillet over medium heat. Add breaded chicken; cook 6 to 8 minutes until browned on both sides. Remove to paper towel-lined plate to drain excess oil.

4 Layer half of eggplant, ¾ cup Parmesan cheese and 1 cup sauce in bottom of **CROCK-POT**® slow cooker. Top with half of chicken, remaining half of eggplant, remaining ¾ cup Parmesan cheese and ¼ cup sauce. Arrange remaining half of chicken on sauce; top with remaining 1 cup sauce and mozzarella cheese. Cover; cook on LOW 6 hours or on HIGH 2 to 4 hours.

MAKES 6 TO 8 SERVINGS

BISTRO CHICKEN IN RICH CREAM SAUCE

4 skinless, bone-in chicken breast halves, rinsed and patted dry (about 3 pounds total)

½ cup dry white wine, divided

1 tablespoon *or* ½ packet (about 1 ounce) Italian salad dressing and seasoning mix

½ teaspoon dried oregano

1 can (10¾ ounces) condensed cream of chicken soup, undiluted

3 ounces cream cheese, cut into cubes

¼ teaspoon salt

⅛ teaspoon black pepper

2 tablespoons chopped fresh Italian parsley (optional)

1 Coat inside of **CROCK-POT®** slow cooker with nonstick cooking spray. Arrange chicken in single layer in bottom, overlapping slightly. Pour ¼ cup wine over chicken. Sprinkle evenly with salad dressing mix and oregano. Cover; cook on LOW 5 to 6 hours or on HIGH 3 hours.

2 Remove chicken to plate with slotted spoon. Whisk soup, cream cheese, salt and pepper into cooking liquid. (Mixture will be a bit lumpy.) Arrange chicken on top. Cover; cook on HIGH 15 to 20 minutes or until heated through.

3 Remove chicken to shallow pasta bowl. Add remaining ¼ cup wine to sauce; whisk until smooth. To serve, spoon sauce around chicken; garnish with parsley.

MAKES 4 SERVINGS

CHICKEN AND MUSHROOM FETTUCCINE ALFREDO

1½ pounds boneless, skinless chicken breasts, cut into 1-inch strips

2 packages (8 ounces *each*) cremini mushrooms, cut into thirds

½ teaspoon salt

¼ teaspoon black pepper

¼ teaspoon garlic powder

2 packages (8 ounces *each*) cream cheese, cut into cubes

1½ cups grated Parmesan cheese, plus additional for garnish

1½ cups whole milk

1 cup (2 sticks) butter, cut into cubes

1 package (1 pound) uncooked fettuccine

Chopped fresh basil (optional)

1 Coat inside of **CROCK-POT**® slow cooker with nonstick cooking spray. Arrange chicken in single layer in bottom of **CROCK-POT**® slow cooker. Top with mushrooms. Sprinkle salt, pepper and garlic powder over mushrooms.

2 Cook and stir cream cheese, 1½ cups Parmesan cheese, milk and butter in medium saucepan over medium heat until smooth and heated through. Pour over mushrooms, pushing down any that float to surface. Cover; cook on LOW 4 to 5 hours or on HIGH 2 to 2½ hours.

3 Cook fettuccine according to package directions. Drain. Add fettuccine to Alfredo sauce and toss gently to combine. Garnish with additional Parmesan cheese and basil.

MAKES 6 TO 8 SERVINGS

CHICKEN SALTIMBOCCA-STYLE

6 boneless, skinless chicken breasts

12 slices prosciutto

12 slices provolone cheese

½ cup all-purpose flour

½ cup grated Parmesan cheese

2 teaspoons salt

2 teaspoons black pepper

Olive oil

2 cans (10¾ ounces *each*) condensed cream of mushroom soup, undiluted

¾ cup dry white wine (optional)

1 teaspoon ground sage

1 Split each chicken breast into two thin pieces. Place between two pieces of waxed paper or plastic wrap; pound until ⅓-inch thick. Place 1 slice of prosciutto and 1 slice of provolone on each chicken piece and roll up. Secure with toothpicks.

2 Combine flour, Parmesan cheese, salt and pepper on large rimmed plate. Dredge chicken in flour mixture, shaking off excess. Reserve excess flour mixture. Heat oil in large skillet over medium heat. Add chicken; cook 5 to 7 minutes or until browned on both sides. Remove to **CROCK-POT**® slow cooker. Add soup, wine, if desired, and sage.

3 Cover; cook on LOW 5 to 7 hours or on HIGH 2 to 3 hours. Remove chicken to large serving platter. Whisk 2 to 3 tablespoons reserved flour mixture into cooking liquid. Cover; cook on HIGH 15 minutes or until thickened. Serve chicken with sauce.

MAKES 6 SERVINGS

COMFORTING
CASSEROLES

WILD RICE AND MUSHROOM CASSEROLE

2 tablespoons olive oil

1 large green bell pepper, finely diced

8 ounces button mushrooms, thinly sliced

½ medium red onion, finely diced

2 cloves garlic, minced

1 can (14 ounces) diced tomatoes, drained

1 teaspoon dried oregano

1 teaspoon paprika

2 tablespoons butter

2 tablespoons all-purpose flour

1½ cups milk

2 cups (8 ounces) shredded pepper jack, Cheddar or Swiss cheese

1 teaspoon salt

½ teaspoon black pepper

2 cups wild rice, cooked according to package directions

Sprigs fresh oregano (optional)

1 Coat inside of **CROCK-POT**® slow cooker with nonstick cooking spray. Heat oil in large skillet over medium heat. Add bell pepper, mushrooms and onion; cook 5 to 6 minutes, stirring occasionally, until vegetables soften. Add garlic, tomatoes, dried oregano and paprika; cook 3 to 5 minutes or until heated through. Remove to large bowl to cool.

2 Melt butter in same skillet over medium heat; whisk in flour. Cook and stir 4 to 5 minutes or until smooth and golden. Whisk in milk; bring to a boil. Whisk in cheese. Season with salt and black pepper.

3 Combine wild rice with vegetables in large bowl. Fold in cheese sauce; mix gently. Pour wild rice mixture into **CROCK-POT**® slow cooker. Cover; cook on LOW 4 to 6 hours or on HIGH 2 to 3 hours. Garnish with oregano sprigs.

MAKES 4 TO 6 SERVINGS

CORNBREAD AND BEAN CASSEROLE

1 medium onion, chopped

1 medium green bell pepper, diced

2 cloves garlic, minced

1 can (about 15 ounces) red kidney beans, rinsed and drained

1 can (about 15 ounces) pinto beans, rinsed and drained

1 can (about 15 ounces) diced tomatoes with mild green chiles

1 can (8 ounces) tomato sauce

1 teaspoon chili powder

½ teaspoon ground cumin

½ teaspoon black pepper

¼ teaspoon hot pepper sauce

1 cup yellow cornmeal

1 cup all-purpose flour

2½ teaspoons baking powder

1 tablespoon sugar

½ teaspoon salt

1¼ cups milk

2 eggs

3 tablespoons vegetable oil

1 can (8½ ounces) cream-style corn

1 Coat inside of **CROCK-POT**® slow cooker with nonstick cooking spray. Heat large skillet over medium heat. Add onion, bell pepper and garlic; cook and stir 5 minutes or until tender. Transfer to **CROCK-POT**® slow cooker.

2 Stir beans, diced tomatoes, tomato sauce, chili powder, cumin, black pepper and hot pepper sauce into **CROCK-POT**® slow cooker. Cover; cook on HIGH 1 hour.

3 Combine cornmeal, flour, baking powder, sugar and salt in large bowl; stir to blend. Stir in milk, eggs and oil; mix well. Stir in corn. Spoon evenly over bean mixture in **CROCK-POT**® slow cooker. Cover; cook on HIGH 1½ to 2 hours or until cornbread topping is golden brown.

MAKES 8 SERVINGS

TIP: Spoon any remaining cornbread topping into greased muffin cups. Bake 30 minutes at 375°F or until golden brown.

HASH BROWN AND SAUSAGE BREAKFAST CASSEROLE

4 cups frozen southern-style hash browns

3 tablespoons unsalted butter

1 large onion, chopped

8 ounces (about 2 cups) sliced mushrooms

3 cloves garlic, minced

2 precooked apple chicken sausages, cut into 1-inch slices

1 package (10 ounces) frozen chopped spinach, thawed and squeezed dry

8 eggs

1 cup milk

1 teaspoon salt

¼ teaspoon black pepper

1½ cups (6 ounces) shredded sharp Cheddar cheese, divided

1 Coat inside of **CROCK-POT®** slow cooker with nonstick cooking spray. Place hash browns in **CROCK-POT®** slow cooker.

2 Melt butter in large skillet over medium-high heat. Add onion, mushrooms and garlic; cook 4 to 5 minutes or until onion is just starting to brown, stirring occasionally. Stir in sausage slices; cook 2 minutes. Add spinach; cook 2 minutes or until mushrooms are tender. Stir sausage mixture into **CROCK-POT®** slow cooker with hash browns until combined.

3 Combine eggs, milk, salt and pepper in large bowl; mix well. Pour over hash brown mixture in **CROCK-POT®** slow cooker. Top with 1 cup cheese. Cover; cook on LOW 4 to 4½ hours or on HIGH 1½ to 2 hours or until eggs are set. Top with remaining ½ cup cheese. Cut into wedges to serve.

MAKES 6 TO 8 SERVINGS

1½ **pounds ground beef**

1 **pound bulk pork sausage**

4 **jars (14 ounces** *each***) pizza sauce**

2 **cups (8 ounces) shredded mozzarella cheese**

2 **cups grated Parmesan cheese**

2 **cans (4 ounces** *each***) mushroom stems and pieces, drained**

2 **packages (3 ounces** *each***) sliced pepperoni**

½ **cup finely chopped onion**

½ **cup finely chopped green bell pepper**

1 **clove garlic, minced**

1 **pound corkscrew pasta, cooked and drained**

1 Brown beef and sausage in large nonstick skillet over medium-high heat 6 to 8 minutes, stirring to break up meat. Drain fat. Remove beef mixture to **CROCK-POT**® slow cooker.

2 Add pizza sauce, cheeses, mushrooms, pepperoni, onion, bell pepper and garlic; stir to blend. Cover; cook on LOW 3½ hours or on HIGH 2 hours.

3 Stir in pasta. Cover; cook on HIGH 15 to 20 minutes or until pasta is heated through.

MAKES 6 SERVINGS

FALL BEEF AND BEER CASSEROLE

2 tablespoons oil

1½ pounds cubed beef stew meat

2 tablespoons all-purpose flour

1 cup beef broth

2 cups brown ale or beer

1 cup water

1 onion, sliced

2 carrots, sliced

1 leek, sliced

2 stalks celery, sliced

1 cup mushrooms, sliced

1 turnip, peeled and cubed

Salt and black pepper

1 Heat oil in large skillet over medium-high heat. Add beef; cook and stir 6 to 8 minutes or until browned on all sides. Remove to **CROCK-POT**® slow cooker.

2 Sprinkle flour over contents of skillet; cook and stir 2 minutes. Gradually stir in broth, ale and water (adding liquid ingredients too fast could create lumps in the sauce). Bring to a boil; pour over beef.

3 Add onion, carrots, leek, celery, mushrooms, turnip, salt and pepper to **CROCK-POT**® slow cooker; stir to blend. Cover; cook on LOW 8 to 10 hours or on HIGH 4 to 6 hours.

MAKES 4 TO 6 SERVINGS

8 ounces pork or turkey Italian sausage, casings removed

½ cup minced onion

1½ cups marinara sauce

1 can (about 14 ounces) Italian-style diced tomatoes

2 packages (9 ounces *each*) refrigerated meatless ravioli, such as wild mushroom or three cheese, divided

1½ cups (6 ounces) shredded mozzarella cheese, divided

Chopped fresh Italian parsley (optional)

1 Heat large skillet over medium-high heat. Brown sausage and onion 6 to 8 minutes, stirring to break up meat. Drain fat. Stir in marinara sauce and tomatoes; mix well. Remove from heat.

2 Coat inside of **CROCK-POT**® slow cooker with nonstick cooking spray. Spoon 1 cup sauce into **CROCK-POT**® slow cooker. Layer half of 1 package of ravioli over sauce; top with additional ½ cup sauce and ½ cup cheese. Repeat layering once; top with ½ cup cheese. Repeat layering with remaining package ravioli and all remaining sauce. Cover; cook on LOW 2½ to 3 hours or on HIGH 1½ to 2 hours or until sauce is heated through and ravioli is tender.

3 Sprinkle remaining ½ cup cheese over top of casserole. Cover; cook on HIGH 15 minutes or until cheese is melted. Garnish with parsley.

MAKES 4 TO 6 SERVINGS

2 cans (10¾ ounces *each*) cream of celery soup

2 cans (5 ounces *each*) tuna in water, drained and flaked

1 cup water

2 carrots, chopped

1 small red onion, chopped

¼ teaspoon black pepper

1 raw egg, uncracked

8 ounces hot cooked egg noodles

Plain dry bread crumbs

2 tablespoons chopped fresh Italian parsley

1 Stir soup, tuna, water, carrots, onion and pepper into **CROCK-POT®** slow cooker. Place whole unpeeled egg on top. Cover; cook on LOW 4 to 5 hours or on HIGH 1½ to 3 hours.

2 Remove egg; stir in pasta. Cover; cook on HIGH 30 to 60 minutes or until onion is tender. Meanwhile, mash egg in small bowl; mix in bread crumbs and parsley. Top casserole with bread crumb mixture.

MAKES 6 SERVINGS

NOTE: This casserole calls for a raw egg. The egg will hard-cook in its shell in the **CROCK-POT®** slow cooker.

HOT THREE-BEAN CASSEROLE

2 tablespoons olive oil

1 cup coarsely chopped onion

1 cup chopped celery

2 cloves garlic, minced

1 can (about 15 ounces) chickpeas, rinsed and drained

1 can (about 15 ounces) kidney beans, rinsed and drained

1 package (10 ounces) frozen cut green beans

1 cup water

1 cup coarsely chopped tomato

1 can (8 ounces) tomato sauce

1 to 2 jalapeño peppers, seeded and minced*

1 tablespoon chili powder

2 teaspoons sugar

1½ teaspoons ground cumin

1 teaspoon salt

1 teaspoon dried oregano

¼ teaspoon black pepper

Sprigs fresh oregano (optional)

*Jalapeño peppers can sting and irritate the skin, so wear rubber gloves when handling peppers and do not touch your eyes.

1 Heat oil in large skillet over medium heat. Add onion, celery and garlic; cook and stir 5 minutes or until tender. Place in **CROCK-POT**® slow cooker.

2 Add chickpeas, beans, water, tomato, tomato sauce, jalapeño pepper, chili powder, sugar, cumin, salt, dried oregano and black pepper to **CROCK-POT**® slow cooker; stir to blend. Cover; cook on LOW 6 to 8 hours. Garnish with fresh oregano.

MAKES 12 SERVINGS

1 can (about 14 ounces) vegetable broth

½ cup cornmeal

1 can (7 ounces) corn, drained

1 can (4 ounces) diced mild green chiles, drained

¼ cup diced red bell pepper

½ teaspoon salt

¼ teaspoon black pepper

1 cup (4 ounces) shredded Cheddar cheese

1 Pour broth into **CROCK-POT®** slow cooker. Whisk in cornmeal. Add corn, chiles, bell pepper, salt and black pepper. Cover; cook on LOW 4 to 5 hours or on HIGH 2 to 3 hours.

2 Stir in cheese. Cook, uncovered, on LOW 15 to 30 minutes or until cheese is melted.

MAKES 6 SERVINGS

TIP: For firmer polenta, divide cooked corn mixture among lightly greased individual ramekins or spread in pie plate. Cover and refrigerate until firm. Serve cold or at room temperature.

BLUEBERRY-ORANGE FRENCH TOAST CASSEROLE

½ cup sugar

½ cup milk

2 eggs

4 egg whites

1 tablespoon grated orange peel

½ teaspoon vanilla

6 slices whole wheat bread, cut into 1-inch cubes

1 cup fresh blueberries

Maple syrup (optional)

1 Coat inside of **CROCK-POT®** slow cooker with nonstick cooking spray. Stir sugar and milk in medium bowl until sugar is dissolved. Whisk in eggs, egg whites, orange peel and vanilla. Add bread and blueberries; stir to coat.

2 Remove mixture to **CROCK-POT®** slow cooker. Cover; cook on LOW 3 to 4 hours or on HIGH 1½ to 2 hours or until toothpick inserted into center comes out mostly clean.

3 Let stand 10 minutes. Serve with syrup, if desired.

MAKES 6 SERVINGS

CERVEZA CHICKEN ENCHILADA CASSEROLE

2 cups water

1 stalk celery, chopped

1 small carrot, chopped

1 can (12 ounces) Mexican beer, divided

   Juice of 1 lime

1 teaspoon salt

1½ pounds boneless, skinless chicken breasts

1 can (19 ounces) enchilada sauce

7 ounces white corn tortilla chips

½ medium onion, chopped

3 cups (12 ounces) shredded Cheddar cheese

   Optional toppings: sour cream, sliced black olives and chopped fresh cilantro

1 Bring water, celery, carrot, 1 cup beer, lime juice and salt to a boil in large saucepan over high heat. Add chicken breasts; reduce heat to simmer. Cook 12 to 14 minutes or until chicken is cooked through. Remove chicken to large cutting board; shred with two forks.

2 Spread ½ cup enchilada sauce in bottom of **CROCK-POT®** slow cooker. Arrange one third of tortilla chips over sauce. Layer with one third of shredded chicken and one third of chopped onion. Sprinkle with 1 cup cheese. Repeat layers two times.

3 Pour remaining beer over casserole. Cover; cook on LOW 3½ to 4 hours. Top as desired.

MAKES 4 TO 6 SERVINGS

LAYERED MEXICAN-STYLE CASSEROLE

2 cans (about 15 ounces *each*) hominy, drained

1 can (about 15 ounces) black beans, rinsed and drained

1 can (about 14 ounces) diced tomatoes with garlic, basil and oregano

1 cup thick and chunky salsa

1 can (6 ounces) tomato paste

½ teaspoon ground cumin

3 (9-inch) flour tortillas

2 cups (8 ounces) shredded Monterey Jack cheese

¼ cup sliced black olives

1 Prepare foil handles by tearing off three 18×2-inch strips of heavy-duty foil or use regular foil folded to double thickness. Crisscross foil strips in spoke design and place in **CROCK-POT**® slow cooker. Coat inside of **CROCK-POT**® slow cooker with nonstick cooking spray. Combine hominy, beans, tomatoes, salsa, tomato paste and cumin in large bowl; stir to blend.

2 Press 1 tortilla in bottom of **CROCK-POT**® slow cooker. Top with one third of hominy mixture and one third of cheese. Repeat layers. Press remaining tortilla on top. Top with remaining hominy mixture. Set aside remaining one third of cheese.

3 Cover; cook on LOW 6 to 8 hours or on HIGH 2 to 3 hours. Turn off heat. Sprinkle with remaining cheese and olives. Cover; let stand 5 minutes. Pull out tortilla stack with foil handles. Cut into six wedges.

MAKES 6 SERVINGS

SWEET POTATO AND PECAN CASSEROLE

1 can (40 ounces) sweet potatoes, drained and mashed

½ cup apple juice

⅓ cup plus 2 tablespoons butter, melted and divided

½ teaspoon salt

½ teaspoon ground cinnamon

¼ teaspoon black pepper

2 eggs, beaten

⅓ cup chopped pecans

⅓ cup packed brown sugar

2 tablespoons all-purpose flour

1 Combine potatoes, apple juice, ⅓ cup butter, salt, cinnamon and pepper in large bowl; beat in eggs. Pour mixture into **CROCK-POT**® slow cooker.

2 Combine pecans, brown sugar, flour and remaining 2 tablespoons butter in small bowl; stir to blend. Spread over sweet potatoes. Cover; cook on HIGH 3 to 4 hours.

MAKES 6 TO 8 SERVINGS

FIVE-BEAN CASSEROLE

2 medium onions, chopped

8 ounces bacon, diced

2 cloves garlic, minced

½ cup packed brown sugar

½ cup cider vinegar

1 teaspoon salt

1 teaspoon dry mustard

¼ teaspoon black pepper

2 cans (about 15 ounces *each*) kidney beans, rinsed and drained

1 can (about 15 ounces) chickpeas, rinsed and drained

1 can (about 15 ounces) butter beans, rinsed and drained

1 can (about 15 ounces) Great Northern or cannellini beans, rinsed and drained

1 can (about 15 ounces) baked beans

Chopped green onions (optional)

1 Heat large nonstick skillet over medium heat. Add onions, bacon and garlic; cook and stir 5 to 7 minutes or until onions are tender. Drain fat. Stir in brown sugar, vinegar, salt, dry mustard and pepper; simmer over low heat 15 minutes.

2 Combine all beans in **CROCK-POT®** slow cooker. Spoon onion mixture evenly over top of beans. Cover; cook on LOW 6 to 8 hours or on HIGH 3 to 4 hours. Serve warm. Garnish each serving with green onions.

MAKES 16 SERVINGS

WAKE-UP POTATO AND SAUSAGE BREAKFAST CASSEROLE

1 pound kielbasa or smoked sausage, diced

1 cup chopped onion

1 cup chopped red bell pepper

1 package (20 ounces) refrigerated Southwestern-style hash browns*

10 eggs

1 cup milk

1 cup (4 ounces) shredded Monterey Jack or sharp Cheddar cheese

*You may substitute O'Brien potatoes and add ½ teaspoon chile pepper.

1 Coat inside of **CROCK-POT**® slow cooker with nonstick cooking spray. Heat large skillet over medium-high heat. Add sausage and onion; cook and stir until sausage is browned. Drain fat. Stir in bell pepper.

2 Place one third of potatoes in **CROCK-POT**® slow cooker. Top with half of sausage mixture. Repeat layers. Spread remaining one third of potatoes evenly on top.

3 Whisk eggs and milk in medium bowl. Pour evenly over potatoes. Cover; cook on LOW 6 to 7 hours.

4 Turn off heat. Sprinkle cheese over casserole; let stand 10 minutes or until cheese is melted.

MAKES 8 SERVINGS

TIP: To remove casserole from **CROCK-POT**® slow cooker, omit step 4. Run a rubber spatula around the edge of casserole, lifting the bottom slightly. Invert onto a large plate. Place a large serving plate on top and invert again. Sprinkle with cheese and let stand until cheese is melted. To serve, cut into wedges.

CHIPOTLE CHICKEN CASSEROLE

1 pound boneless, skinless chicken thighs, cut into cubes

1½ cups chicken broth

1 can (about 15 ounces) navy beans, rinsed and drained

1 can (about 15 ounces) black beans, rinsed and drained

1 can (about 14 ounces) crushed tomatoes, undrained

½ cup orange juice

1 medium onion, diced

1 canned chipotle pepper in adobo sauce, minced

1 teaspoon salt

1 teaspoon ground cumin

1 whole bay leaf

Combine chicken, broth, beans, tomatoes, orange juice, onion, chipotle pepper, salt, cumin and bay leaf in **CROCK-POT®** slow cooker; stir to blend. Cover; cook on LOW 7 to 8 hours or on HIGH 3½ to 4 hours. Remove and discard bay leaf before serving.

MAKES 6 SERVINGS

MOM'S TUNA CASSEROLE

2 cans (12 ounces *each*) solid albacore tuna, drained and flaked

3 cups diced celery

3 cups crushed potato chips, divided

6 hard-cooked eggs, chopped

1 can (10½ ounces) condensed cream of mushroom soup, undiluted

1 can (10½ ounces) condensed cream of celery soup, undiluted

1 cup mayonnaise

1 teaspoon dried tarragon

1 teaspoon black pepper

1 Combine tuna, celery, 2½ cups potato chips, eggs, soups, mayonnaise, tarragon and pepper in **CROCK-POT®** slow cooker; stir to blend. Cover; cook on LOW 5 to 7 hours.

2 Sprinkle with remaining ½ cup potato chips before serving.

MAKES 8 SERVINGS

TIP: Don't use your **CROCK-POT®** slow cooker to reheat leftover foods. Remove cooled leftover food to a resealable food storage bag or storage container with a tight-fitting lid and refrigerate. Use a microwave oven, the stove top or the oven for reheating.

CHICKEN AND WILD RICE CASSEROLE

3 tablespoons olive oil

2 slices bacon, chopped

1½ pounds chicken thighs, trimmed

½ cup diced onion

½ cup diced celery

2 tablespoons Worcestershire sauce

½ teaspoon salt

¼ teaspoon black pepper

½ teaspoon dried sage

1 cup uncooked converted long grain white rice

1 package (4 ounces) wild rice

6 ounces brown mushrooms, wiped clean and quartered*

3 cups hot chicken broth**

2 tablespoons chopped fresh Italian parsley (optional)

*Use "baby bellas" or cremini mushrooms. Or you may substitute white button mushrooms.

**Use enough broth to cover chicken.

1 Spread oil on bottom of **CROCK-POT**® slow cooker. Microwave bacon on HIGH 1 minute. Remove to **CROCK-POT**® slow cooker. Place chicken in **CROCK-POT**® slow cooker, skin side down. Add onion, celery, Worcestershire sauce, salt, pepper, sage, white rice, wild rice, mushrooms and broth. Cover; cook on LOW 3 to 4 hours or until rice is tender.

2 Turn off heat. Uncover; let stand 15 minutes before serving. Remove chicken skin, if desired. Garnish with chopped parsley.

MAKES 4 TO 6 SERVINGS

CHEESY BROCCOLI CASSEROLE

2 packages (10 ounces each) frozen chopped broccoli, thawed

1 can (10½ ounces) condensed cream of celery soup, undiluted

1¼ cups (5 ounces) shredded sharp Cheddar cheese, divided

¼ cup minced onion

1 teaspoon paprika

1 teaspoon hot pepper sauce

½ teaspoon celery seeds

1 cup crushed potato chips or saltine crackers

1 Coat inside of **CROCK-POT**® slow cooker with nonstick cooking spray. Combine broccoli, soup, 1 cup cheese, onion, paprika, hot pepper sauce and celery seeds in **CROCK-POT**® slow cooker; stir to blend. Cover; cook on LOW 5 to 6 hours or on HIGH 2½ to 3 hours.

2 Uncover; sprinkle top with potato chips and remaining ¼ cup cheese. Cook, uncovered, on LOW 30 to 60 minutes or on HIGH 15 to 30 minutes or until cheese is melted.

MAKES 4 TO 6 SERVINGS

VARIATIONS: Substitute thawed chopped spinach for the broccoli and top with spicy croutons.

GREEN BEAN CASSEROLE

2 packages (10 ounces *each*) frozen green beans

1 can (10¾ ounces) condensed cream of mushroom soup, undiluted

1 tablespoon chopped fresh Italian parsley

1 tablespoon chopped roasted red peppers

1 teaspoon dried sage

½ teaspoon salt

½ teaspoon black pepper

¼ teaspoon ground nutmeg

½ cup toasted slivered almonds*

*To toast almonds, spread in single layer in small heavy skillet. Cook and stir over medium heat 1 to 2 minutes or until nuts are lightly browned.

Combine beans, soup, parsley, red peppers, sage, salt, black pepper and nutmeg in **CROCK-POT®** slow cooker; stir to blend. Cover; cook on LOW 3 to 4 hours. Sprinkle with almonds.

MAKES 6 SERVINGS

DOWN-HOME SQUASH CASSEROLE

4 cups corn bread stuffing
   mix (half of 16-ounce
   package)

½ cup (1 stick) butter,
   melted

1 can (10¾ ounces)
   condensed cream of
   chicken soup,
   undiluted

¾ cup mayonnaise

¼ cup milk

¼ teaspoon poultry
   seasoning or rubbed
   sage

3 medium yellow squash,
   cut into ½-inch slices
   (about 1 pound total)

1½ cups frozen seasoning
   blend vegetables,
   thawed*

*Seasoning blend is a mixture of
chopped bell peppers, onions and celery.
If seasoning blend is unavailable, use
½ cup *each* of fresh vegetables.

1 Coat inside of **CROCK-POT**® slow cooker with nonstick cooking spray. Combine stuffing and butter in large bowl; toss gently to coat stuffing thoroughly. Place two thirds of stuffing in **CROCK-POT**® slow cooker. Place remaining stuffing on plate; set aside.

2 Combine soup, mayonnaise, milk and poultry seasoning in same large bowl. Add squash and vegetables; stir until coated thoroughly. Pour mixture over stuffing mix in **CROCK-POT**® slow cooker. Top evenly with reserved stuffing. Cover; cook on LOW 4 hours or until squash is tender.

3 Turn off heat. Uncover; let stand 15 minutes before serving.

MAKES 8 TO 10 SERVINGS

BEEFY MAIN DISHES

CAJUN POT ROAST

1 boneless beef chuck roast (3 pounds)*

1 to 2 tablespoons Cajun seasoning

1 tablespoon vegetable oil

1 can (about 14 ounces) diced tomatoes

1 can (about 14 ounces) diced tomatoes with mild green chiles

1 medium onion, chopped

1 cup chopped rutabaga

1 cup chopped mushrooms

1 cup chopped turnip

1 cup chopped parsnip

1 cup chopped green bell pepper

1 cup green beans

1 cup sliced carrots

1 cup corn

2 tablespoons hot pepper sauce

1 teaspoon sugar

½ teaspoon black pepper

¾ cup water

*Unless you have a 5-, 6- or 7-quart **CROCK-POT**® slow cooker, cut any roast larger than 2½ pounds in half so it cooks completely.

1 Coat inside of **CROCK-POT**® slow cooker with nonstick cooking spray. Season roast with cajun seasoning. Heat oil in large skillet over medium-high heat. Brown roast 5 minutes on each side.

2 Place roast, tomatoes, onion, rutabaga, mushrooms, turnip, parsnip, bell pepper, green beans, carrots, corn, hot pepper sauce, sugar and black pepper in **CROCK-POT**® slow cooker. Pour in water. Cover; cook on LOW 6 hours.

MAKES 6 SERVINGS

BEEFY TOSTADA PIE

2 teaspoons olive oil

1½ cups chopped onion

2 pounds ground beef

1 teaspoon salt

1 teaspoon ground cumin

1 teaspoon chili powder

2 cloves garlic, minced

1 can (15 ounces) tomato sauce

1 cup sliced black olives

8 (6-inch) flour tortillas

3½ cups (14 ounces) shredded Cheddar cheese

Sour cream and chopped green onion (optional)

1 Heat oil in large skillet over medium heat. Add onion; cook and stir 3 to 5 minutes or until tender. Add beef, salt, cumin, chili powder and garlic; cook and stir 6 to 8 minutes or until beef is browned. Drain fat. Stir in tomato sauce; cook until heated through. Stir in olives.

2 Make foil handles using three 18×2-inch strips of heavy-duty foil or use regular foil folded to double thickness. Crisscross foil in spoke design; place across bottom and up side of **CROCK-POT®** slow cooker. Lay 1 tortilla on foil strips. Spread with meat sauce and ½ cup cheese. Top with another tortilla, meat sauce and cheese. Repeat layers five times, ending with tortilla. Cover; cook on HIGH 1½ hours.

3 To serve, lift out of **CROCK-POT®** slow cooker using foil handles and remove to large serving platter. Discard foil. Cut into wedges. Serve with sour cream and green onion, if desired.

MAKES 4 TO 6 SERVINGS

CORNED BEEF AND CABBAGE

2 onions, thickly sliced

1 corned beef brisket (about 3 pounds) with seasoning packet

1 package (8 to 10 ounces) baby carrots

6 medium potatoes, cut into wedges

1 cup water

3 to 5 slices bacon

1 head green cabbage, cut into wedges

1 Place onions in bottom of **CROCK-POT**® slow cooker. Add corned beef with seasoning packet, carrots and potato wedges. Pour 1 cup water over top. Cover; cook on LOW 10 hours.

2 With 30 minutes left in cooking time, heat large saucepan over medium heat. Add bacon; cook and stir until crisp. Remove to paper towel-lined plate using slotted spoon. Reserve drippings in pan. Crumble bacon when cool enough to handle.

3 Place cabbage in saucepan with bacon drippings, cover with water. Bring to a boil; cook 20 to 30 minutes or until cabbage in tender. Drain. Serve corned beef with vegetables; topped with bacon.

MAKES 6 SERVINGS

SHEPHERD'S PIE

1 pound ground beef

1 pound ground lamb

1 package (12 ounces) frozen chopped onions

2 teaspoons minced garlic

1 package (16 ounces) frozen peas and carrots

1 can (about 14 ounces) diced tomatoes, drained

3 tablespoons quick-cooking tapioca

2 teaspoons dried oregano

1 teaspoon salt

½ teaspoon black pepper

2 packages (24 ounces *each*) prepared mashed potatoes

1 Brown beef and lamb in large nonstick skillet over medium-high heat 6 to 8 minutes, stirring to break up meat. Remove to **CROCK-POT**® slow cooker using slotted spoon. Wipe out skillet with paper towel; return to medium heat. Add onions and garlic; cook and stir until onions are tender. Remove to **CROCK-POT**® slow cooker.

2 Stir peas and carrots, tomatoes, tapioca, oregano, salt and pepper into **CROCK-POT**® slow cooker. Cover; cook on LOW 7 to 8 hours.

3 Top with prepared mashed potatoes. Cover; cook on LOW 30 minutes or until potatoes are heated through.

MAKES 6 SERVINGS

BRISKET WITH SWEET ONIONS

2 large sweet onions, cut into 10 (½-inch) slices*

1 flat-cut boneless beef brisket (about 3½ pounds)

Salt and black pepper

2 cans (about 14 ounces *each*) beef broth

1 teaspoon cracked black peppercorns

¾ cup crumbled blue cheese (optional)

*Preferably Maui, Vidalia or Walla Walla onions.

1 Coat inside of **CROCK-POT**® slow cooker with nonstick cooking spray. Line bottom with onion slices.

2 Season brisket with salt and black pepper. Heat large skillet over medium-high heat. Add brisket; cook 10 to 12 minutes or until browned on all sides. Remove to **CROCK-POT**® slow cooker.

3 Pour broth into **CROCK-POT**® slow cooker. Sprinkle brisket with peppercorns. Cover; cook on HIGH 5 to 7 hours.

4 Remove brisket to large cutting board. Cover loosely with foil; let stand 10 to 15 minutes before slicing. To serve, arrange onions on serving platter and spread slices of brisket on top. Sprinkle with blue cheese, if desired. Serve with cooking liquid.

MAKES 10 SERVINGS

BURGUNDY BEEF PO' BOYS WITH DIPPING SAUCE

1 boneless beef chuck shoulder or bottom round roast (about 3 pounds), trimmed*

2 cups chopped onions

¼ cup dry red wine

3 tablespoons balsamic vinegar

1 tablespoon beef bouillon granules

1 tablespoon Worcestershire sauce

¾ teaspoon dried thyme

½ teaspoon garlic powder

Italian rolls, warmed and split

*Unless you have a 5-, 6- or 7-quart **CROCK-POT®** slow cooker, cut any roast larger than 2½ pounds in half so it cooks completely.

1 Cut beef into 3 to 4 pieces. Place onions in bottom of **CROCK-POT®** slow cooker. Top with beef, wine, vinegar, bouillon granules, Worcestershire sauce, thyme and garlic powder. Cover; cook on HIGH 8 to 10 hours.

2 Remove beef from **CROCK-POT®** slow cooker to large cutting board; shred with two forks. Let cooking liquid stand 5 minutes. Skim off any fat and discard. Spoon beef onto rolls. Serve with cooking liquid as dipping sauce.

MAKES 6 TO 8 SERVINGS

1 can (10¾ ounces) condensed cream of mushroom soup, undiluted

1 package (about 1 ounce) dry onion soup mix

1 boneless beef chuck shoulder roast (3 to 5 pounds)*

4 to 5 medium potatoes, unpeeled and quartered

4 cups baby carrots

*Unless you have a 5-, 6- or 7-quart **CROCK-POT®** slow cooker, cut any roast larger than 2½ pounds in half so it cooks completely.

1 Combine mushroom soup and dry soup mix in **CROCK-POT®** slow cooker; stir to blend. Place roast in **CROCK-POT®** slow cooker. Cover; cook on LOW 4 hours.

2 Stir in potatoes and carrots. Cover; cook on LOW 2 hours.

MAKES 6 TO 8 SERVINGS

BACON, ONION AND STOUT BRAISED SHORT RIBS

4 pounds bone-in beef short ribs, well trimmed

1 teaspoon salt, plus additional for seasoning

½ teaspoon black pepper, plus additional for seasoning

1 tablespoon vegetable oil

6 ounces thick-cut bacon, cut into ¼-inch slices

1 large onion, halved and cut into ¼-inch slices

2 tablespoons all-purpose flour

2 tablespoons spicy brown mustard

1 tablespoon tomato paste

1 can (12 ounces) Irish stout

1 whole bay leaf

1 cup beef broth

2 tablespoons finely chopped fresh Italian parsley

Hot mashed potatoes or cooked egg noodles (optional)

1 Season beef with salt and pepper. Heat oil in large skillet over medium-high heat until almost smoking. Add short ribs in batches, cook 5 to 7 minutes or until browned on all sides. Remove to **CROCK-POT®** slow cooker.

2 Wipe out skillet with paper towels and return to heat. Add bacon; cook and stir until crisp. Remove to paper towel-lined plate using slotted spoon. Remove and discard all but 1 tablespoon drippings from pan. Reduce heat to medium. Add onion; cook and stir 5 to 7 minutes or until softened. Add flour, mustard, tomato paste, 1 teaspoon salt and ½ teaspoon pepper; cook and stir 1 minute. Remove skillet from heat; pour in stout, stirring to scrape any browned bits from bottom of skillet. Pour stout mixture over short ribs. Add bacon, bay leaf and broth to **CROCK-POT®** slow cooker. Cover; cook on LOW 8 hours.

3 Turn off heat. Remove beef to large serving platter. Let cooking liquid stand 5 minutes. Skim off and discard fat. Remove and discard bay leaf. Stir in parsley. Serve with mashed potatoes, if desired.

MAKES 4 TO 6 SERVINGS

CHEESEBURGER SLOPPY JOES

1½ pounds ground beef

3 cloves garlic, minced

1 small onion, chopped

½ cup ketchup

¼ cup water

1 tablespoon packed
brown sugar

1 teaspoon
Worcestershire sauce

2 cups (8 ounces)
shredded sharp
Cheddar cheese

6 to 8 hamburger rolls

Carrot and celery sticks
(optional)

1 Coat inside of **CROCK-POT**® slow cooker with nonstick cooking spray. Brown beef in large skillet over medium-high heat 6 to 8 minutes, stirring to break up meat. Remove beef to **CROCK-POT**® slow cooker using slotted spoon. Wipe out skillet with paper towels; return to heat. Stir in garlic and onion; cook and stir 3 to 4 minutes.

2 Add garlic, onion, ketchup, water, brown sugar and Worcestershire sauce to **CROCK-POT**® slow cooker; stir to blend. Cover; cook on LOW 4 to 5 hours or on HIGH 2 to 2½ hours. Stir in cheese until melted. Serve on rolls with carrot and celery sticks, if desired.

MAKES 6 TO 8 SERVINGS

BEEF AND VEAL MEAT LOAF

1 tablespoon olive oil

1 small onion, chopped

½ red bell pepper, chopped

3 cloves garlic, minced

1 teaspoon dried oregano

1 pound ground beef

1 pound ground veal

1 egg

3 tablespoons tomato paste

1 teaspoon salt

½ teaspoon black pepper

1 Coat inside of **CROCK-POT®** slow cooker with nonstick cooking spray. Heat oil in large skillet over medium-high heat. Add onion, bell pepper, garlic and oregano; cook and stir 5 minutes or until vegetables are softened. Remove onion mixture to large bowl; cool 6 minutes.

2 Add beef, veal, egg, tomato paste, salt and black pepper; mix well. Form into 9×5-inch loaf; place in **CROCK-POT®** slow cooker. Cover; cook on LOW 5 to 6 hours. Remove meat loaf to large cutting board; let stand 10 minutes before slicing.

MAKES 6 SERVINGS

POT ROAST WITH BACON AND MUSHROOMS

6 slices bacon

1 boneless beef chuck roast (2½ to 3 pounds), trimmed*

¾ teaspoon salt, divided

¼ teaspoon black pepper

¾ cup chopped shallots

8 ounces sliced white mushrooms

¼ ounce dried porcini mushrooms (optional)

4 cloves garlic, minced

1 teaspoon dried oregano

1 cup chicken broth

2 tablespoons tomato paste

Roasted Cauliflower (recipe follows, optional)

*Unless you have a 5-, 6- or 7-quart **CROCK-POT**® slow cooker, cut any roast larger than 2½ pounds in half so it cooks completely.

1 Heat large skillet over medium heat. Add bacon; cook and stir until crisp. Remove to paper towel-lined plate using slotted spoon; crumble.

2 Pour off all but 2 tablespoons fat from skillet. Season roast with ½ teaspoon salt and pepper. Heat same skillet over medium-high heat. Add roast; cook 8 minutes or until well browned. Remove to large plate. Add shallots, white mushrooms, porcini mushrooms, if desired, garlic, oregano and remaining ¼ teaspoon salt; cook 3 to 4 minutes or until softened. Remove shallot mixture to **CROCK-POT**® slow cooker.

3 Stir bacon into **CROCK-POT**® slow cooker. Place roast on top of vegetables. Combine broth and tomato paste in small bowl; stir to blend. Pour broth mixture over roast. Cover; cook on LOW 8 hours. Remove roast to large cutting board. Let stand 10 minutes before slicing. Top each serving with vegetables and cooking liquid. Serve with Roasted Cauliflower, if desired.

MAKES 6 TO 8 SERVINGS

ROASTED CAULIFLOWER: Preheat oven to 375°F. Break 1 head cauliflower into florets onto large baking sheet; coat with olive oil. Roast 20 minutes. Turn; roast 15 minutes. Makes 6 servings.

BEEF AND QUINOA STUFFED CABBAGE ROLLS

8 large green cabbage leaves, veins trimmed at bottom of each leaf

1 pound ground beef

1½ cups cooked quinoa

1 medium onion, chopped

1 cup tomato juice, divided

Salt and black pepper

1 Heat salted water in large saucepan over high heat; bring to a boil. Add cabbage leaves; return to boil. Cook 2 minutes. Drain and let cool.

2 Combine beef, quinoa, onion, ¼ cup tomato juice, salt and pepper in large bowl; mix well. Place cabbage leaf on large work surface; top center with 2 to 3 tablespoons beef mixture. Starting at stem end, roll up jelly-roll style, folding sides in as you go. Repeat with remaining cabbage rolls and beef mixture.

3 Place cabbage rolls seam side down and side by side in single layer in **CROCK-POT**® slow cooker. Pour in remaining ¾ cup tomato juice. Cover; cook on LOW 5 to 6 hours.

MAKES 4 SERVINGS

EASY SALISBURY STEAK

1½ **pounds ground beef**

1 **egg**

½ **cup plain dry bread crumbs**

1 **package (about 1 ounce) onion soup mix***

1 **can (10½ ounces) golden mushroom soup, undiluted**

*You may pulse onion soup mix in a small food processor or coffee grinder for a finer grind, if desired.

1 Coat inside of **CROCK-POT®** slow cooker with nonstick cooking spray. Combine beef, egg, bread crumbs and dry soup mix in large bowl. Form mixture evenly into four 1-inch thick patties.

2 Heat large skillet over medium-high heat. Add patties; cook 2 minutes per side until lightly browned. Remove to **CROCK-POT®** slow cooker, in single layer. Spread mushroom soup evenly over patties. Cover; cook on LOW 3 to 3½ hours.

MAKES 4 SERVINGS

BACON AND ONION BRISKET

6 slices bacon, cut crosswise into ½-inch slices

1 flat-cut boneless beef brisket (about 2½ pounds)

Salt and black pepper

3 medium onions, sliced

2 cans (10½ ounces *each*) condensed beef broth, undiluted

1 Heat large skillet over medium heat. Add bacon; cook and stir until crisp. Remove to **CROCK-POT®** slow cooker using slotted spoon.

2 Season brisket with salt and pepper. Add to skillet; cook 5 to 7 minutes on each side or until browned on all sides. Remove to **CROCK-POT®** slow cooker.

3 Reduce skillet heat to medium-low. Add onions; cook and stir 3 to 5 minutes or until softened. Add to **CROCK-POT®** slow cooker. Pour in broth. Cover; cook on HIGH 6 to 8 hours or until meat is tender.

4 Remove brisket to large cutting board. Cover loosely with foil; let stand 10 minutes. Slice brisket against the grain into thin slices. Spoon bacon, onions and cooking liquid over brisket to serve.

MAKES 6 SERVINGS

MEATBALLS AND SPAGHETTI SAUCE

2 pounds ground beef

1 cup plain dry bread crumbs

1 onion, chopped

2 eggs, beaten

¼ cup minced fresh Italian parsley

4 teaspoons minced garlic, divided

½ teaspoon dry mustard

½ teaspoon black pepper

4 tablespoons olive oil, divided

1 can (28 ounces) whole tomatoes

½ cup chopped fresh basil

1 teaspoon sugar

Salt and black pepper

Hot cooked spaghetti

1 Combine beef, bread crumbs, onion, eggs, parsley, 2 teaspoons garlic, dry mustard and ½ teaspoon pepper in large bowl. Form into walnut-sized balls. Heat 2 tablespoons oil in large skillet over medium heat. Brown meatballs on all sides. Remove to **CROCK-POT**® slow cooker.

2 Combine tomatoes, basil, remaining 2 tablespoons oil, 2 teaspoons garlic, sugar, salt and black pepper in medium bowl; stir to blend. Pour over meatballs; turn to coat. Cover; cook on LOW 3 to 5 hours or on HIGH 2 to 4 hours. Serve over spaghetti.

MAKES 6 TO 8 SERVINGS

TIP: Recipe can be doubled for a 5-, 6- or 7-quart **CROCK-POT**® slow cooker.

DELICIOUS PEPPER STEAK

2 tablespoons toasted sesame oil

2 pounds beef round steak, cut into strips

½ medium red bell pepper, sliced

½ medium green bell pepper, sliced

½ medium yellow bell pepper, sliced

1 medium onion, sliced

14 grape tomatoes

⅓ cup hoisin sauce

¼ cup water

3 tablespoons all-purpose flour

3 tablespoons soy sauce

2 teaspoons garlic powder

1 teaspoon ground cumin

1 teaspoon dried oregano

1 teaspoon paprika

⅛ teaspoon ground red pepper

Hot cooked rice (optional)

1 Heat oil in large skillet over medium-high heat. Add beef in batches; cook 4 to 5 minutes or until browned. Remove to large paper towel-lined plate.

2 Add bell peppers, onion and tomatoes to **CROCK-POT®** slow cooker. Combine hoisin sauce, water, flour, soy sauce, garlic powder, cumin, oregano, paprika and ground red pepper in medium bowl; stir to blend. Add to **CROCK-POT®** slow cooker. Add beef. Cover; cook on LOW 8 to 9 hours or on HIGH 4 to 4½ hours. Serve with rice, if desired.

MAKES 6 SERVINGS

½ cup paprika

¼ cup sugar

¼ cup onion powder

1½ teaspoons salt

1½ teaspoons black pepper

2½ pounds beef ribs, cut into 3 to 4 sections

1 can (20 ounces) beer or beef broth

1 quart barbecue sauce

½ cup honey

Sesame seeds and fresh chopped chives (optional)

1 Combine paprika, sugar, onion powder, salt and pepper in small bowl; stir to blend. Season ribs with dry rub mixture. Heat large skillet over medium-high heat. Add ribs; cook 3 minutes on each side or until browned.

2 Place in **CROCK-POT®** slow cooker. Pour beer over ribs. Cover; cook on HIGH 2 hours. Combine barbecue sauce and honey in medium bowl; add to **CROCK-POT®** slow cooker. Cover; cook on HIGH 1½ hours. Sprinkle with sesame seeds and chives, if desired. Serve with extra sauce.

MAKES 6 TO 8 SERVINGS

NEW ENGLAND CHUCK ROAST

- 1 boneless beef chuck roast (4 to 5 pounds), string on*
- 2 teaspoons salt
- ¼ teaspoon black pepper
  Olive oil
- 4 cups water, divided
- 2 cups carrots, cut into 2-inch pieces
- 1½ cups yellow onion, cut into quarters
- 4 small red potatoes, cut into quarters
- 2 stalks celery, cut into 1-inch pieces
- 3 whole bay leaves
- 2 tablespoons white vinegar
- 2 tablespoons prepared horseradish
- 1 head cabbage, cut into quarters or eighths
- 4 tablespoons all-purpose flour
- 2 tablespoons cornstarch

*Unless you have a 5-, 6- or 7-quart **CROCK-POT**® slow cooker, cut any roast larger than 2½ pounds in half so it cooks completely.

1 Season roast with salt and pepper. Heat oil in large skillet over medium heat. Brown roast on all sides. Remove to **CROCK-POT**® slow cooker.

2 Add 3 cups water, carrots, onion, potatoes, celery, bay leaves, vinegar and horseradish. Cover; cook on LOW 5 to 7 hours or on HIGH 2 to 4 hours.

3 One hour before serving, add cabbage to **CROCK-POT**® slow cooker. Stir remaining 1 cup water into flour and cornstarch in medium bowl until smooth. Whisk flour mixture into **CROCK-POT**® slow cooker. Cover; cook on HIGH 1 hour or until thickened. Remove and discard bay leaves. Remove roast to large cutting board. Cover loosely with foil; let stand 10 to 15 minutes. Remove and discard string. Slice roast; serve with sauce and vegetables.

MAKES 8 SERVINGS

CLASSIC BEEF AND NOODLES

1 tablespoon vegetable oil

2 pounds cubed beef stew meat

¼ pound mushrooms, sliced into halves

2 tablespoons chopped onion

2 cloves garlic, minced

1 teaspoon salt

1 teaspoon dried oregano

½ teaspoon black pepper

¼ teaspoon dried marjoram

1 whole bay leaf

1½ cups beef broth

⅓ cup dry sherry

1 container (8 ounces) sour cream

½ cup all-purpose flour

¼ cup water

4 cups hot cooked noodles

1 Heat oil in large skillet over medium heat. Brown beef in batches on all sides. Drain fat.

2 Combine beef, mushrooms, onion, garlic, salt, oregano, pepper, marjoram and bay leaf in **CROCK-POT**® slow cooker. Pour in broth and sherry. Cover; cook on LOW 8 to 10 hours or on HIGH 4 to 5 hours. Remove and discard bay leaf.

3 Combine sour cream, flour and water in small bowl. Stir about 1 cup cooking liquid from **CROCK-POT**® slow cooker into sour cream mixture. Whisk mixture into **CROCK-POT**® slow cooker. Cook, uncovered, on HIGH 30 minutes or until thickened and bubbly. Serve over noodles.

MAKES 8 SERVINGS

BEST BEEF BRISKET SANDWICH EVER

1 beef brisket (about 3 pounds)*

2 cups apple cider, divided

1 head garlic, cloves separated, crushed and peeled

⅓ cup chopped fresh thyme *or* 2 tablespoons dried thyme

2 tablespoons whole black peppercorns

1 tablespoon mustard seeds

1 tablespoon Cajun seasoning

1 teaspoon ground allspice

1 teaspoon ground cumin

1 teaspoon celery seeds

2 to 4 whole cloves

1 can (12 ounces) dark beer

10 to 12 sourdough sandwich rolls, sliced in half

10 to 12 slice Swiss cheese

*Unless you have a 5-, 6- or 7-quart **CROCK-POT**® slow cooker, cut any roast larger than 2½ pounds in half so it cooks completely.

1 Place brisket, ½ cup cider, garlic, thyme, peppercorns, mustard seeds, Cajun seasoning, allspice, cumin, celery seeds and cloves in large resealable food storage bag. Seal bag; turn to coat. Marinate in refrigerator overnight.

2 Place brisket and marinade in **CROCK-POT**® slow cooker. Add remaining 1½ cups cider and beer. Cover; cook on LOW 10 hours or until brisket is tender.

3 Slice brisket and place on sandwich rolls. Strain sauce; drizzle over meat. Top with cheese.

MAKES 10 TO 12 SERVINGS

BRAISED SHORT RIBS WITH AROMATIC SPICES

1 tablespoon olive oil

3 pounds bone-in beef short ribs, trimmed

1 teaspoon ground cumin, divided

1 teaspoon salt

½ teaspoon black pepper

2 medium onions, halved and thinly sliced

10 cloves garlic, thinly sliced

2 tablespoons balsamic vinegar

2 tablespoons honey

1 whole cinnamon stick

2 whole star anise pods

2 large sweet potatoes, peeled and cut into ¾-inch cubes

1 cup beef broth

1 Heat oil in large skillet over medium-high heat. Season ribs with ½ teaspoon cumin, salt and pepper. Add to skillet; cook 8 minutes or until browned, turning occasionally. Remove ribs to large plate.

2 Heat same skillet over medium heat. Add onions and garlic; cook 12 to 14 minutes or until onions are lightly browned. Stir in vinegar; cook 1 minute. Add remaining ½ teaspoon cumin, honey, cinnamon stick and star anise; cook and stir 30 seconds. Remove mixture to **CROCK-POT®** slow cooker. Stir in potatoes; top with ribs. Pour in broth.

3 Cover; cook on LOW 8 to 9 hours or until meat is falling off the bones. Remove and discard bones from ribs. Remove and discard cinnamon stick and star anise. Turn off heat. Let mixture stand 5 to 10 minutes. Skim off and discard fat. Serve meat with sauce and vegetables.

MAKES 4 SERVINGS

ON THE SIDE

ASIAGO AND ASPARAGUS RISOTTO-STYLE RICE

2 cups chopped onion

1 can (about 14 ounces) vegetable broth

1 cup uncooked converted rice

2 cloves garlic, minced

½ pound asparagus spears, trimmed and broken into 1-inch pieces

1 cup half-and-half, divided

½ cup (about 4 ounces) grated Asiago cheese, plus additional for garnish

¼ cup (½ stick) butter, cubed

½ cup (2 ounces) pine nuts or slivered almonds, toasted*

1 teaspoon salt

*To toast nuts, spread in single layer in heavy skillet. Cook over medium heat 1 to 2 minutes or until nuts are lightly browned, stirring frequently.

1 Place onion, broth, rice and garlic into **CROCK-POT**® slow cooker; stir until well blended. Cover; cook on HIGH 2 hours or until rice is tender.

2 Stir in asparagus and ½ cup half-and-half. Cover; cook on HIGH 20 minutes or until asparagus is crisp-tender.

3 Stir in remaining ½ cup half-and-half, ½ cup cheese, butter, pine nuts and salt. Turn off heat. Cover; let stand 5 minutes or until cheese is slightly melted. Fluff with fork. Garnish with additional cheese.

MAKES 4 SERVINGS

TIP: Risotto is a classic creamy rice dish of northern Italy and can be made with a wide variety of ingredients. Fresh vegetables and cheeses such as Asiago work especially well in risotto. Parmesan cheese, shellfish, white wine and herbs are also popular additions.

SWISS CHEESE SCALLOPED POTATOES

2 pounds baking potatoes, thinly sliced

½ cup finely chopped yellow onion

¼ teaspoon salt

¼ teaspoon ground nutmeg

2 tablespoons butter, cut into small pieces

½ cup milk

2 tablespoons all-purpose flour

¾ cup (3 ounces) shredded Swiss cheese

¼ cup finely chopped green onions

1 Layer half of potatoes, ¼ cup onion, ⅛ teaspoon salt, ⅛ teaspoon nutmeg and 1 tablespoon butter in **CROCK-POT®** slow cooker. Repeat layers. Cover; cook on LOW 7 hours or on HIGH 4 hours.

2 Remove potatoes with slotted spoon to serving dish; keep warm.

3 Whisk milk into flour in small bowl until smooth; stir into cooking liquid. Stir in cheese. Cover; cook on HIGH 10 minutes or until slightly thickened. Stir; pour cheese mixture over potatoes. Sprinkle with green onions.

MAKES 5 TO 6 SERVINGS

RUSTIC GARLIC MASHED POTATOES

2 pounds baking potatoes, unpeeled and cut into ½-inch cubes

¼ cup water

2 tablespoons unsalted butter, cut into cubes

1¼ teaspoons salt

½ teaspoon garlic powder

¼ teaspoon black pepper

1 cup milk

Place potatoes, water, butter, salt, garlic powder and pepper in **CROCK-POT**® slow cooker; toss to combine. Cover; cook on LOW 7 hours or on HIGH 4 hours. Add milk to potatoes. Mash potatoes with potato masher until smooth.

MAKES 5 SERVINGS

HOMESTYLE MAC 'N' CHEESE

12 ounces uncooked elbow macaroni (about 3 cups)

2 cans (12 ounces *each*) evaporated milk

1 cup milk

⅓ cup all-purpose flour

¼ cup (½ stick) unsalted butter, melted

2 eggs, lightly beaten

1 teaspoon dry mustard

½ teaspoon salt

¼ teaspoon black pepper

4 cups (16 ounces) shredded sharp Cheddar cheese

Toasted plain dry bread crumbs (optional)

1 Coat inside of **CROCK-POT®** slow cooker with nonstick cooking spray. Bring large saucepan of lightly salted water to a boil. Add macaroni to saucepan; cook according to package directions. Drain. Remove to **CROCK-POT®** slow cooker.

2 Combine evaporated milk, milk, flour, butter, eggs, dry mustard, salt and pepper in large bowl; stir to blend. Pour into **CROCK-POT®** slow cooker. Stir in cheese until well combined. Cover; cook on LOW 3½ to 4 hours or until cheese is melted and macaroni is heated through. Stir well. Top each serving with bread crumbs, if desired.

MAKES 6 TO 8 SERVINGS

BUTTERMILK CORN BREAD

1½ cups cornmeal

½ cup all-purpose flour

1 tablespoon sugar

2 teaspoons baking powder

½ teaspoon salt

1½ cups buttermilk

½ teaspoon baking soda

2 eggs

¼ cup (½ stick) butter, melted

¼ cup chopped seeded jalapeño peppers*

1 tablespoon finely chopped pimientos or roasted red pepper

*Jalapeño peppers can sting and irritate the skin, so wear rubber gloves when handling peppers and do not touch your eyes.

1 Coat inside of **CROCK-POT®** slow cooker with nonstick cooking spray.

2 Sift cornmeal, flour, sugar, baking powder and salt into large bowl. Whisk buttermilk into baking soda in medium bowl. Add eggs to buttermilk mixture; whisk lightly until blended. Stir in butter.

3 Stir buttermilk mixture, jalapeño peppers and pimientos into cornmeal mixture until just blended. *Do not overmix.* Pour into **CROCK-POT®** slow cooker. Cover; cook on HIGH 1½ to 2 hours.

MAKES 1 LOAF

LEMON-MINT RED POTATOES

2 pounds new red potatoes

3 tablespoons extra virgin olive oil

1 teaspoon salt

½ teaspoon Greek seasoning or dried oregano

¼ teaspoon garlic powder

¼ teaspoon black pepper

4 tablespoons chopped fresh mint, divided

2 tablespoons butter

2 tablespoons lemon juice

1 teaspoon grated lemon peel

1 Coat inside of **CROCK-POT**® slow cooker with nonstick cooking spray. Add potatoes and oil, stirring gently to coat. Sprinkle with salt, Greek seasoning, garlic powder and pepper. Cover; cook on LOW 7 hours or on HIGH 4 hours.

2 Stir in 2 tablespoons mint, butter, lemon juice and lemon peel until butter is completely melted. Cover; cook on HIGH 15 minutes. Sprinkle with remaining 2 tablespoons mint.

MAKES 4 SERVINGS

TIP: It's easy to prepare these potatoes ahead of time. Simply follow the recipe and then turn off the heat. Let it stand at room temperature for up to 2 hours. You may reheat or serve the potatoes at room temperature.

FIVE-INGREDIENT MUSHROOM STUFFING

6 tablespoons unsalted butter

2 medium onions, chopped

1 pound sliced white mushrooms

¼ teaspoon salt

5 cups bagged stuffing mix, any seasoning

1 cup vegetable broth

Chopped fresh Italian parsley (optional)

1 Melt butter in large skillet over medium-high heat. Add onions, mushrooms and salt; cook and stir 20 minutes or until vegetables are browned and most liquid is absorbed. Remove onion mixture to **CROCK-POT**® slow cooker.

2 Stir in stuffing mix and broth. Cover; cook on LOW 3 hours. Garnish with parsley.

MAKES 12 SERVINGS

NO-FUSS MACARONI AND CHEESE

2 cups (about 8 ounces) uncooked elbow macaroni

3 ounces light pasteurized processed cheese product, cubed

1 cup (4 ounces) shredded mild Cheddar cheese

½ teaspoon salt

⅛ teaspoon black pepper

1½ cups milk

Combine macaroni, cheese product, cheese, salt and pepper in **CROCK-POT®** slow cooker. Pour milk over top. Cover; cook on LOW 2 to 3 hours, stirring halfway through cooking time.

MAKES 8 SERVINGS

MUSHROOM AND ROMANO RISOTTO

3 tablespoons extra virgin olive oil

8 ounces sliced mushrooms

½ cup chopped shallots

½ cup chopped onion

3 cloves garlic, minced

1½ cups uncooked Arborio rice

½ cup Madeira wine

4½ cups vegetable broth

½ cup Romano cheese

3 tablespoons butter

3 tablespoons chopped fresh Italian parsley

¼ teaspoon black pepper

1 Heat oil in large skillet over medium-high heat. Add mushrooms; cook and stir 6 to 7 minutes or until mushrooms begin to brown. Stir in shallots, onion and garlic; cook and stir 2 to 3 minutes or until vegetables begin to soften. Add rice; cook and stir 1 minute. Add Madeira; cook and stir 1 minute or until almost absorbed.

2 Remove mixture to **CROCK-POT**® to slow cooker. Add broth. Cover; cook on HIGH 2 hours or until liquid is absorbed and rice is tender.

3 Turn off heat. Stir in cheese, butter, parsley and pepper.

MAKES 4 SERVINGS

CURRIED POTATOES, CAULIFLOWER AND PEAS

1 tablespoon vegetable oil

1 onion, chopped

2 tablespoons minced fresh ginger

2 cloves garlic, chopped

2 pounds red potatoes, cut into ½-inch-thick rounds

1 teaspoon garam masala*

1 teaspoon salt

1 small (about 1¼ pounds) head cauliflower, trimmed and broken into florets

1 cup vegetable broth

2 ripe plum (Roma) tomatoes, seeded and chopped

1 cup thawed frozen peas

Hot cooked basmati or long grain rice

*Garam masala is a blend of Asian spices available in the spice aisle of many supermarkets. If garam masala is unavailable substitute ½ teaspoon ground cumin and ½ teaspoon ground coriander seeds.

1 Heat oil in large skillet over medium heat. Add onion, ginger and garlic; cook and stir 5 to 7 minutes or until onion is softened. Remove from heat; set aside.

2 Put potatoes in **CROCK-POT®** slow cooker. Mix garam masala and salt in small bowl. Sprinkle half of spice mixture over potatoes. Top with onion mixture, then cauliflower. Sprinkle remaining spice mixture over cauliflower. Pour in broth. Cover; cook on HIGH 3½ hours.

3 Remove cover and gently stir in tomatoes and peas. Cover; cook on HIGH 30 minutes or until potatoes are tender. Stir gently. Spoon over rice in bowls to serve.

MAKES 6 SERVINGS

ANGELIC DEVILED EGGS

6 eggs

¼ cup cottage cheese

3 tablespoons ranch dressing

2 teaspoons Dijon mustard

2 tablespoons minced fresh chives or dill

1 tablespoon diced well-drained pimientos or roasted red pepper

1 Place eggs in single layer in bottom of **CROCK-POT**® slow cooker; add just enough water to cover tops of eggs. Cover; cook on LOW 3½ hours. Rinse and drain eggs under cold water; peel when cool enough to handle.

2 Cut eggs in half lengthwise. Remove yolks, reserving 3 yolk halves. Discard remaining yolks or reserve for another use. Place egg whites, cut sides up, on serving plate; cover with plastic wrap. Refrigerate while preparing filling.

3 Combine cottage cheese, dressing, mustard and reserved yolk halves in food processor or blender; process until smooth. (Or, place in small bowl and mash with fork until well blended.) Remove cheese mixture to small bowl; stir in chives and pimientos. Spoon into egg whites. Cover and refrigerate at least 1 hour before serving.

MAKES 12 SERVINGS

SCALLOPED POTATOES AND PARSNIPS

6 tablespoons butter

3 tablespoons all-purpose flour

1½ cups whipping cream

2 teaspoons ground mustard

1½ teaspoons salt

1 teaspoon dried thyme

½ teaspoon black pepper

2 baking potatoes, peeled, cut in half lengthwise, then crosswise into ¼-inch slices

2 parsnips, cut into ¼-inch slices

1 onion, chopped

2 cups (8 ounces) shredded sharp Cheddar cheese

1 Melt butter in medium saucepan over medium-high heat. Whisk in flour; cook 1 to 2 minutes. Gradually whisk in cream until smooth. Stir in mustard, salt, thyme and pepper.

2 Place potatoes, parsnips and onion in **CROCK-POT®** slow cooker. Add cream sauce. Cover; cook on LOW 7 hours or on HIGH 3½ hours or until potatoes are tender.

3 Turn off heat. Stir in cheese. Cover; let stand until cheese is melted.

MAKES 4 TO 6 SERVINGS

MASHED ROOT VEGETABLES

1 pound baking potatoes, peeled and cut into 1-inch pieces

1 pound turnips, peeled and cut into 1-inch pieces

12 ounces sweet potatoes, peeled and cut into 1-inch pieces

8 ounces parsnips, peeled and cut into ½-inch pieces

5 tablespoons butter

¼ cup water

2 teaspoons salt

¼ teaspoon black pepper

1 cup milk

1 Coat inside of **CROCK-POT®** slow cooker with nonstick cooking spray. Add baking potatoes, turnips, sweet potatoes, parsnips, butter, water, salt and pepper; stir to blend. Cover; cook on HIGH 3 to 4 hours.

2 Mash mixture with potato masher until smooth. Stir in milk. Cover; cook on HIGH 15 minutes.

MAKES 6 SERVINGS

BLUE CHEESE POTATOES

2 pounds red potatoes, peeled and cut into ½-inch pieces

1¼ cups chopped green onions, divided

2 tablespoons olive oil, divided

1 teaspoon dried basil

½ teaspoon salt

¼ teaspoon black pepper

½ cup crumbled blue cheese

1 Layer potatoes, 1 cup green onions, 1 tablespoon oil, basil, salt and pepper in **CROCK-POT®** slow cooker. Cover; cook on LOW 7 hours or on HIGH 4 hours.

2 Gently stir in cheese and remaining 1 tablespoon oil. Cover; cook on HIGH 5 minutes. Remove potatoes to large serving platter; top with remaining ¼ cup green onions.

MAKES 5 SERVINGS

CREAMY BARLEY RISOTTO

3 cups vegetable broth

1 cup uncooked pearl barley

1 large leek, white and light green parts thinly sliced, separated into rings

1 cup frozen baby peas

1 tablespoon lemon juice

1 teaspoon grated lemon peel, plus additional for garnish

2 tablespoons butter, cut into 4 pieces

Salt and black pepper

Shaved Parmesan cheese (optional)

Chopped fresh Italian parsley (optional)

1 Coat inside of **CROCK-POT**® slow cooker with nonstick cooking spray. Combine broth, barley and leek in **CROCK-POT**® slow cooker. Cover; cook on LOW 4 to 5 hours or on HIGH 2 to 2½ hours or until most liquid is absorbed.

2 Stir in peas, lemon juice and 1 teaspoon lemon peel. Cover; cook on HIGH 10 minutes or until heated through. Stir in butter until melted. Season with salt and pepper. Garnish with Parmesan cheese, parsley and additional lemon peel.

.MAKES 4 SERVINGS

SPINACH GORGONZOLA CORN BREAD

- 2 boxes (8½ ounces *each*) corn bread mix
- 1 box (10 ounces) frozen chopped spinach, thawed and drained
- 1 cup crumbled Gorgonzola cheese
- 3 eggs
- ½ cup whipping cream
- 1 teaspoon black pepper
- Paprika (optional)

1 Coat inside of 5-quart **CROCK-POT**® slow cooker with nonstick cooking spray. Combine corn bread mix, spinach, cheese, eggs, cream, pepper and paprika, if desired, in medium bowl; stir to blend. Place batter in **CROCK-POT**® slow cooker.

2 Cover; cook on HIGH 1½ hours. Turn off heat. Let bread cool completely before inverting onto large serving platter.

MAKES 1 LOAF

NOTE: Cook only on HIGH setting for proper crust and texture.

CHORIZO AND CORN BREAD DRESSING

½ pound chorizo sausage, casings removed

1 can (about 14 ounces) chicken broth

1 can (10¾ ounces) condensed cream of chicken soup, undiluted

1 cup chopped onion

1 cup diced red bell pepper

1 cup chopped celery

1 cup frozen corn

1 box (6 ounces) corn bread stuffing mix

3 eggs, lightly beaten

1 Coat inside of **CROCK-POT**® slow cooker with nonstick cooking spray. Heat large skillet over medium-high heat. Brown sausage 6 to 8 minutes, stirring to break up meat. Remove to **CROCK-POT**® slow cooker using slotted spoon; return skillet to heat.

2 Whisk broth and soup into drippings in skillet. Add onion, bell pepper, celery, corn, stuffing mix and eggs; stir until well blended. Stir broth mixture into **CROCK-POT**® slow cooker. Cover; cook on LOW 7 hours or on HIGH 3½ hours.

MAKES 4 TO 6 SERVINGS

SLOW-COOKED SUCCOTASH

2 teaspoons olive oil

1 cup diced onion

1 cup diced green bell pepper

1 cup diced celery

1 teaspoon paprika

1½ cups frozen corn

1½ cups frozen lima beans

1 cup canned diced tomatoes

2 teaspoons dried parsley flakes *or* 1 tablespoon minced fresh Italian parsley

Salt and black pepper

1 Heat oil in large skillet over medium heat. Add onion, bell pepper and celery; cook and stir 5 minutes or until vegetables are crisp-tender. Stir in paprika.

2 Stir onion mixture, corn, beans, tomatoes, parsley flakes, salt and black pepper into **CROCK-POT**® slow cooker. Cover; cook on LOW 6 to 8 hours or on HIGH 3 to 4 hours.

MAKES 8 SERVINGS

GRATIN POTATOES WITH ASIAGO CHEESE

6 slices bacon, cut into
   1-inch pieces

6 medium baking
   potatoes, peeled and
   thinly sliced

½ cup grated Asiago
   cheese

   Salt and black pepper

1½ cups whipping cream

1 Heat large skillet over medium heat. Add bacon; cook and stir until crisp. Remove to paper towel-lined plate using slotted spoon.

2 Pour bacon drippings into **CROCK-POT**® slow cooker. Layer one fourth of potatoes on bottom of **CROCK-POT**® slow cooker. Sprinkle one fourth of bacon over potatoes and top with one fourth of cheese. Season with salt and pepper.

3 Repeat layers three times. Pour cream over all. Cover; cook on LOW 7 to 9 hours or on HIGH 5 to 6 hours.

MAKES 4 TO 6 SERVINGS

SATISFYING
SWEETS

BANANAS FOSTER

12 bananas, cut into quarters

1 cup flaked coconut

1 cup dark corn syrup

⅔ cup butter, melted

¼ cup lemon juice

2 teaspoons grated lemon peel

2 teaspoons rum

1 teaspoon ground cinnamon

½ teaspoon salt

12 slices prepared pound cake

1 quart vanilla ice cream

1 Combine bananas and coconut in **CROCK-POT**® slow cooker. Combine corn syrup, butter, lemon juice, lemon peel, rum, cinnamon and salt in medium bowl; stir to blend. Pour over bananas.

2 Cover; cook on LOW 1 to 2 hours. To serve, arrange bananas on pound cake slices. Top with ice cream and warm sauce.

MAKES 12 SERVINGS

PUMPKIN BREAD PUDDING

2 cups whole milk

½ cup (1 stick) plus
    2 tablespoons butter,
    divided

1 cup packed brown sugar,
    divided

1 cup canned solid-pack
    pumpkin

3 eggs

1 tablespoon ground
    cinnamon

2 teaspoons vanilla

½ teaspoon ground
    nutmeg

¼ teaspoon salt

16 slices cinnamon raisin
    bread, torn into small
    pieces (8 cups total)

½ cup whipping cream

2 tablespoons bourbon
    (optional)

1 Coat inside of **CROCK-POT**® slow cooker with nonstick cooking spray. Combine milk and 2 tablespoons butter in medium microwavable bowl. Microwave on HIGH 2½ to 3 minutes or until very warm.

2 Whisk ½ cup brown sugar, pumpkin, eggs, cinnamon, vanilla, nutmeg and salt in large bowl until well blended. Whisk in milk mixture until blended. Add bread cubes; toss to coat.

3 Remove bread mixture to **CROCK-POT**® slow cooker. Cover; cook on HIGH 2 hours or until knife inserted in center comes out clean. Turn off heat. Uncover; let stand 15 minutes.

4 Combine remaining ½ cup butter, remaining ½ cup brown sugar and cream in small saucepan; bring to a boil over high heat, stirring frequently. Remove from heat. Stir in bourbon, if desired. Spoon bread pudding into individual bowls; top with sauce.

MAKES 8 SERVINGS

DULCE DE LECHE

1 can (14 ounces) sweetened condensed milk

1 Pour milk into 9×5-inch loaf pan. Cover tightly with foil. Place loaf pan in **CROCK-POT®** slow cooker. Pour enough water to reach halfway up sides of loaf pan. Cover; cook on LOW 5 to 6 hours or until golden and thickened.

2 Coat inside of **CROCK-POT® LITTLE DIPPER®** slow cooker with nonstick cooking spray. Fill with warm dip.

MAKES ABOUT 1½ CUPS

SERVING SUGGESTION: Try this Dulce de Leche as a fondue with bananas, apples, shortbread, chocolate wafers, pretzels and/or waffle cookies.

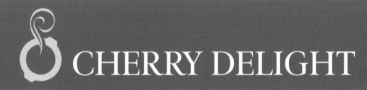

CHERRY DELIGHT

1 **can (21 ounces) cherry pie filling**

1 **package (about 18 ounces) yellow cake mix**

½ **cup (1 stick) butter, melted**

⅓ **cup chopped walnuts**

Place pie filling in **CROCK-POT®** slow cooker. Combine cake mix and butter in medium bowl. Spread evenly over pie filling. Sprinkle with walnuts. Cover; cook on LOW 3 to 4 hours or on HIGH 1½ to 2 hours.

MAKES 8 TO 10 SERVINGS

FUDGE AND CREAM PUDDING CAKE

2 tablespoons unsalted butter

1 cup all-purpose flour

½ cup packed light brown sugar

5 tablespoons unsweetened cocoa powder, divided

2 teaspoons baking powder

½ teaspoon ground cinnamon

⅛ teaspoon salt

1 cup light cream

1 tablespoon vegetable oil

1 teaspoon vanilla

1½ cups hot water

½ cup packed dark brown sugar

Whipped cream (optional)

1 Coat inside of 5-quart **CROCK-POT®** slow cooker with butter. Combine flour, light brown sugar, 3 tablespoons cocoa, baking powder, cinnamon and salt in medium bowl. Add cream, oil and vanilla; stir to blend. Pour batter into **CROCK-POT®** slow cooker.

2 Combine hot water, dark brown sugar and remaining 2 tablespoons cocoa in medium bowl; stir well. Pour sauce over cake batter. *Do not stir.* Cover; cook on HIGH 2 hours. Serve with whipped cream, if desired.

MAKES 8 TO 10 SERVINGS

APPLE CRUMBLE POT

4 Granny Smith apples (about 2 pounds), cored and *each* cut into 8 wedges

1 cup packed dark brown sugar, divided

½ cup dried cranberries

1 cup plus 2 tablespoons biscuit baking mix, divided

2 tablespoons butter, cubed

1½ teaspoons ground cinnamon, plus additional for topping

1 teaspoon vanilla

¼ teaspoon ground allspice

½ cup rolled oats

3 tablespoons cold butter, cubed

½ cup chopped pecans

Whipped cream (optional)

1 Coat inside of **CROCK-POT**® slow cooker with nonstick cooking spray. Combine apples, ⅔ cup brown sugar, cranberries, 2 tablespoons baking mix, 2 tablespoons butter, 1½ teaspoons cinnamon, vanilla and allspice in **CROCK-POT**® slow cooker; toss gently to coat.

2 Combine remaining 1 cup baking mix, oats and remaining ⅓ cup brown sugar in large bowl. Cut in 3 tablespoons cold butter with pastry blender or two knives until mixture resembles coarse crumbs. Sprinkle evenly over filling in **CROCK-POT**® slow cooker. Top with pecans. Cover; cook on HIGH 2¼ hours or until apples are tender. *Do not overcook.*

3 Turn off heat. Let stand, uncovered, 15 to 30 minutes before serving. Top with whipped cream sprinkled with additional cinnamon, if desired.

MAKES 6 TO 8 SERVINGS

MEXICAN CHOCOLATE BREAD PUDDING

1½ cups whipping cream

4 ounces unsweetened chocolate, coarsely chopped

½ cup currants

2 eggs, beaten

½ cup sugar

1 teaspoon vanilla

¾ teaspoon ground cinnamon, plus additional for topping

½ teaspoon ground allspice

⅛ teaspoon salt

3 cups Hawaiian-style sweet bread, challah or rich egg bread, cut into ½-inch cubes

Whipped cream (optional)

1 Heat cream in large saucepan. Add chocolate; stir until melted.

2 Combine currants, eggs, sugar, vanilla, ¾ teaspoon cinnamon, allspice and salt in medium bowl; stir to blend. Add currant mixture to chocolate mixture; stir well to combine. Pour into **CROCK-POT**® slow cooker.

3 Gently fold in bread cubes using plastic spatula. Cover; cook on HIGH 3 to 4 hours or until knife inserted near center comes out clean.

4 Serve warm or chilled. Top with whipped cream sprinkled with additional cinnamon, if desired.

MAKES 6 TO 8 SERVINGS

RUSTIC PEACH-OAT CRUMBLE

8 cups frozen sliced peaches, thawed and juice reserved

¾ cup packed brown sugar, divided

1½ tablespoons cornstarch

1 tablespoon lemon juice (optional)

1½ teaspoons vanilla

½ teaspoon almond extract

1 cup quick oats

¼ cup all-purpose flour

¼ cup granulated sugar

1 teaspoon ground cinnamon

¼ teaspoon salt

½ cup (1 stick) cold butter, cubed

1 Coat inside of 5-quart **CROCK-POT**® slow cooker with nonstick cooking spray. Combine peaches with juice, ½ cup brown sugar, cornstarch, lemon juice, if desired, vanilla and almond extract in medium bowl; toss to coat. Place in **CROCK-POT**® slow cooker.

2 Combine oats, flour, remaining ¼ cup brown sugar, granulated sugar, cinnamon and salt in medium bowl. Cut in butter with pastry blender or two knives until mixture resembles coarse crumbs. Sprinkle over peaches. Cover; cook on HIGH 1½ hours or until bubbly at edge. Remove stoneware to wire rack; let cool 20 minutes.

MAKES ABOUT 8 SERVINGS

ROCKY ROAD BROWNIE BOTTOMS

½ **cup packed brown sugar**

½ **cup water**

2 **tablespoons unsweetened cocoa powder**

2½ **cups packaged brownie mix**

1 **package (about 4 ounces) instant chocolate pudding mix**

½ **cup milk chocolate chips**

2 **eggs, beaten**

3 **tablespoons butter, melted**

2 **cups mini marshmallows**

1 **cup chopped pecans or walnuts, toasted***

½ **cup chocolate syrup**

*To toast pecans, spread in a single layer on small baking sheet. Bake in preheated 350°F oven 5 to 7 minutes or until fragrant, stirring frequently.

1 Coat inside of **CROCK-POT**® slow cooker with nonstick cooking spray. Combine brown sugar, water and cocoa in small saucepan over medium heat; bring to a boil over medium-high heat.

2 Meanwhile, combine brownie mix, pudding mix, chocolate chips, eggs and butter in medium bowl; stir until well blended. Spread batter in **CROCK-POT**® slow cooker; pour boiling sugar mixture over batter.

3 Cover; cook on HIGH 1½ hours. Turn off heat. Top brownies with marshmallows, pecans and chocolate syrup. Let stand 15 minutes.

MAKES 6 SERVINGS

NOTE: Recipe can be doubled for a 5-, 6- or 7-quart **CROCK-POT**® slow cooker.

MIXED BERRY COBBLER

1 package (16 ounces) frozen mixed berries

½ cup granulated sugar

2 tablespoons quick-cooking tapioca

2 teaspoons grated lemon peel

1½ cups all-purpose flour

½ cup packed light brown sugar

2¼ teaspoons baking powder

¼ teaspoon ground nutmeg

½ cup milk

⅓ cup butter, melted

Vanilla ice cream (optional)

1 Coat inside of **CROCK-POT®** slow cooker with nonstick cooking spray. Stir berries, granulated sugar, tapioca and lemon peel in medium bowl. Remove to **CROCK-POT®** slow cooker.

2 Combine flour, brown sugar, baking powder and nutmeg in medium bowl. Add milk and butter; stir just until blended. Drop spoonfuls of dough on top of berry mixture. Cover; cook on LOW 4 hours. Turn off heat. Uncover; let stand 30 minutes. Serve with ice cream, if desired.

MAKES 8 SERVINGS

TIP: Cobblers are year-round favorites. Experiment with seasonal fresh fruits, such as pears, plums, peaches, rhubarb, blueberries, raspberries, strawberries, blackberries or gooseberries.

CRAN-CHERRY BREAD PUDDING

1½ cups light cream

3 egg yolks, beaten

⅓ cup sugar

¼ teaspoon kosher salt

1½ teaspoons cherry extract

⅔ cup dried sweetened cranberries

⅔ cup golden raisins

½ cup whole candied red cherries, halved

½ cup dry sherry

9 cups unseasoned stuffing mix

1 cup white chocolate baking chips

Whipped cream (optional)

1 Prepare foil handles by tearing off three 18×3-inch strips heavy foil (or use regular foil folded to double thickness). Crisscross foil strips in spoke design; place in **CROCK-POT®** slow cooker. Spray 2-quart baking dish that fits inside of **CROCK-POT®** slow cooker with nonstick cooking spray.

2 Cook and stir cream, egg yolks, sugar and salt in medium heavy saucepan over medium heat until mixture coats back of spoon. Remove from heat. Set saucepan in bowl of ice water; stir to cool. Stir in cherry extract. Remove to bowl; press plastic wrap onto surface of custard; refrigerate.

3 Combine cranberries, raisins and cherries in small bowl. Heat sherry in small saucepan until warm. Pour over fruit; let stand 10 minutes.

4 Fold stuffing mix and baking chips into custard. Drain fruit, reserving sherry; stir into custard. Pour into prepared dish. Top with reserved sherry; cover tightly with foil. Place on foil handles in **CROCK-POT®** slow cooker. Add water to come 1 inch up side of dish.

5 Cover; cook on LOW 3½ to 5½ hours or until pudding springs back when touched. Carefully remove dish using foil handles; uncover and let stand 10 minutes. Serve warm with whipped cream, if desired.

MAKES 12 SERVINGS

TRIPLE CHOCOLATE FANTASY

2 pounds white almond bark, broken into pieces

1 bar (4 ounces) sweetened chocolate, broken into pieces*

1 package (12 ounces) semisweet chocolate chips

2 cups coarsely chopped pecans, toasted**

*Use your favorite high-quality chocolate candy bar.

**To toast pecans, spread in single layer in heavy skillet. Cook and stir over medium heat 1 to 2 minutes or until nuts are lightly browned.

1 Line mini muffin pan with liners. Place bark, sweetened chocolate and chocolate chips in **CROCK-POT**® slow cooker. Cover; cook on HIGH 1 hour. *Do not stir.*

2 Turn **CROCK-POT**® slow cooker to LOW. Cover; cook on LOW 1 hour, stirring every 15 minutes. Stir in nuts.

3 Drop mixture by tablespoonfuls into prepared muffin pan; cool completely. Store in tightly covered container.

MAKES 36 PIECES

VARIATIONS: Here are a few ideas for other imaginative items to add in along with or instead of the pecans: raisins, crushed peppermint candy, candy-coated baking bits, crushed toffee, peanuts or pistachio nuts, chopped gum drops, chopped dried fruit, candied cherries, chopped marshmallows or sweetened coconut.

CINNAMON ROLL-TOPPED MIXED BERRY COBBLER

2 bags (12 ounces *each*) frozen mixed berries, thawed

1 cup sugar

¼ cup quick-cooking tapioca

¼ cup water

2 teaspoons vanilla

1 package (about 12 ounces) refrigerated cinnamon rolls with icing

Combine berries, sugar, tapioca, water and vanilla in **CROCK-POT®** slow cooker; top with cinnamon rolls. Cover; cook on LOW 4 to 5 hours. Serve warm; drizzled with icing.

MAKES 8 SERVINGS

NOTE: This recipe was designed to work best in a 4-quart **CROCK-POT®** slow cooker. Double the ingredients for larger **CROCK-POT®** slow cookers, but always place cinnamon rolls in a single layer.

8 cups bread, cubed

3 cups Granny Smith apples, cubed

1 cup chopped pecans

8 eggs

1 can (12 ounces) evaporated milk

1 cup packed brown sugar

½ cup apple cider or apple juice

2 teaspoons ground cinnamon

1 teaspoon ground nutmeg

1 teaspoon vanilla

½ teaspoon salt

½ teaspoon ground allspice

Ice cream (optional)

Caramel topping (optional)

1 Coat inside of **CROCK-POT**® slow cooker with nonstick cooking spray. Add bread cubes, apples and pecans.

2 Combine eggs, evaporated milk, brown sugar, apple cider, cinnamon, nutmeg, vanilla, salt and allspice in large bowl; whisk to blend. Pour egg mixture into **CROCK-POT**® slow cooker. Cover; cook on LOW 3 hours. Serve with ice cream topped with caramel sauce, if desired.

MAKES 8 SERVINGS

PINEAPPLE RICE PUDDING

1 can (20 ounces) crushed pineapple in juice, undrained

1 can (13½ ounces) unsweetened coconut milk

1 can (12 ounces) evaporated milk

¾ cup uncooked Arborio rice

2 eggs, lightly beaten

¼ cup granulated sugar

¼ cup packed brown sugar

½ teaspoon ground cinnamon

¼ teaspoon salt

¼ teaspoon ground nutmeg

Toasted coconut and pineapple slices (optional)*

*To toast coconut, spread in single layer in small heavy-bottomed skillet. Cook and stir over medium heat 1 to 2 minutes or until lightly browned. Remove from skillet immediately.

1 Combine crushed pineapple with juice, coconut milk, evaporated milk, rice, eggs, granulated sugar, brown sugar, cinnamon, salt and nutmeg in **CROCK-POT®** slow cooker; stir to blend. Cover; cook on HIGH 3 to 4 hours or until thickened and rice is tender.

2 Stir to blend. Serve warm or chilled. Top with toasted coconut and pineapple slices, if desired.

MAKES 8 SERVINGS

DECADENT CHOCOLATE DELIGHT

1 package (about 18 ounces) chocolate cake mix

1 container (8 ounces) sour cream

1 cup semisweet chocolate chips

1 cup water

4 eggs

½ cup vegetable oil

1 package (4-serving size) instant chocolate pudding and pie filling mix

Vanilla ice cream (optional)

1 Coat inside of **CROCK-POT**® slow cooker with nonstick cooking spray.

2 Combine cake mix, sour cream, chocolate chips, water, eggs, oil and pie filling mix in medium bowl; stir to blend. Remove to **CROCK-POT**® slow cooker.

3 Cover; cook on LOW 3 to 4 hours or on HIGH 1½ to 1¾ hours. Serve warm with ice cream, if desired.

MAKES 12 SERVINGS

METRIC CONVERSION CHART

VOLUME MEASUREMENTS (dry)

1/8 teaspoon = 0.5 mL
1/4 teaspoon = 1 mL
1/2 teaspoon = 2 mL
3/4 teaspoon = 4 mL
1 teaspoon = 5 mL
1 tablespoon = 15 mL
2 tablespoons = 30 mL
1/4 cup = 60 mL
1/3 cup = 75 mL
1/2 cup = 125 mL
2/3 cup = 150 mL
3/4 cup = 175 mL
1 cup = 250 mL
2 cups = 1 pint = 500 mL
3 cups = 750 mL
4 cups = 1 quart = 1 L

VOLUME MEASUREMENTS (fluid)

1 fluid ounce (2 tablespoons) = 30 mL
4 fluid ounces (1/2 cup) = 125 mL
8 fluid ounces (1 cup) = 250 mL
12 fluid ounces (1 1/2 cups) = 375 mL
16 fluid ounces (2 cups) = 500 mL

WEIGHTS (mass)

1/2 ounce = 15 g
1 ounce = 30 g
3 ounces = 90 g
4 ounces = 120 g
8 ounces = 225 g
10 ounces = 285 g
12 ounces = 360 g
16 ounces = 1 pound = 450 g

DIMENSIONS

1/16 inch = 2 mm
1/8 inch = 3 mm
1/4 inch = 6 mm
1/2 inch = 1.5 cm
3/4 inch = 2 cm
1 inch = 2.5 cm

OVEN TEMPERATURES

250°F = 120°C
275°F = 140°C
300°F = 150°C
325°F = 160°C
350°F = 180°C
375°F = 190°C
400°F = 200°C
425°F = 220°C
450°F = 230°C

BAKING PAN SIZES

Utensil	Size in Inches/Quarts	Metric Volume	Size in Centimeters
Baking or Cake Pan (square or rectangular)	8×8×2	2 L	20×20×5
	9×9×2	2.5 L	23×23×5
	12×8×2	3 L	30×20×5
	13×9×2	3.5 L	33×23×5
Loaf Pan	8×4×3	1.5 L	20×10×7
	9×5×3	2 L	23×13×7
Round Layer Cake Pan	8×1½	1.2 L	20×4
	9×1½	1.5 L	23×4
Pie Plate	8×1¼	750 mL	20×3
	9×1¼	1 L	23×3
Baking Dish or Casserole	1 quart	1 L	—
	1½ quart	1.5 L	—
	2 quart	2 L	—